STUDY GUIDE

KENRICK S. THOMPSON, Ph.D.

SOCIAL PROBLEMS

THIRTEENTH EDITION

William Kornblum

Joseph Julian

PEARSON
Prentice Hall

Upper Saddle River, New Jersey 07458

Upper Saddle River, New Jersey 07458

10 9 8 7 6 5 4 3 2 1

ISBN 13: 978-0-13-601649-6
ISBN 10: 0-13-601649-9

Printed in the United States of America

CONTENTS

PREFACE

This study guide is designed to accompany *Social Problems,* 13th edition, by William Kornblum and Joseph Julian. It is designed to facilitate an understanding of key theories, concepts, research and analysis in the text and can be used as a study aid to prepare for exams.
Each chapter in the study guide is divided into six sections, which are as follows:

- Learning Objectives: This list should help the student focus on the major concepts and points discussed in the chapter.
- Chapter Outline: The detailed outline is designed to help students recall the major topics discussed in the chapter
- Key Terms: This section provides a list of the bold-faced terms in the chapter.
- Chapter Summary: This provides a brief overview of the content of the entire chapter.
- Research Navigator Exercises: This section is designed to help students explore additional topics related to material in the text, and to assist students in becoming familiar with online research. Your text will provide you with a Research Navigator code so that you can log on to the Prentice Hall Research Navigator Website. This website allows access to Content Select, an online library of scholarly journals; the *New York Times* Online; and Links Library, which provides links to relevant websites. For Content Select and *New York Times*, keywords and specific articles are provided, followed by thought-provoking questions that ask students to go beyond what they have read. Finally, directions indicate how to use Link Library to locate Web sites with information relevant to each chapter; again, questions ask students to go beyond what they have read.
- Practice Tests: Twenty multiple choice questions allow students to self-test their comprehension of chapter content. Several essay questions allow students the opportunity to interpret and synthesize what they have learned.

KST

CHAPTER ONE

Sociological Perspectives on Social Problems

CHAPTER OUTLINE

I. What Is a Social Problem?
II. Perspectives on Social Problems
    A. The Functionalist Perspective
        1. Criminal Deviance: A Functionalist View
        2. Social Problems as Social Pathology
        3. Social-Disorganization Theory
        4. Modern Functionalism: Building Institutions
    B. The Conflict Perspective
        1. Deviance: A Marxist Conflict View
        2. Value Conflict Theory
        3. Is There a Culture War in the United States?
    C. The Interactionist Perspective
        1. Labeling: An Interactionist View of Deviance
        2. The Social Construction of Social Problems
III. The Natural History of Social Problems
IV. The Media and Social Problems
V. Research on Social Problems
    A. Demographic Studies
    B. Survey Research
    C. Field Observation
    D. Social Experiments
VI. Social Policy
    A. Future Prospects
VII. Going Beyond Left and Right
VIII. Summary
IX. Key Terms
X. Social Problems Online
XI. Research Navigator

LEARNING OBJECTIVES

After reading Chapter One you should:

1. Be able to define a social problem and be able to illustrate the key components of the definition with examples.
2. Be familiar with the three major theoretical perspectives on social problems, understand the major transitions in functionalist thinking, know the distinction between Marxist and value conflict theory, and understand the interactionist/labeling perspective.
3. Understand the "natural history" approach to social problems and know the stages that most social problems go through.

4. Be familiar with the role played by the media in defining and developing ideas about social problems.
5. Understand the major research methods used to study and analyze social problems, including demographic studies, surveys, field work, and social experiments.
6. Understand the concept of social policy and how policy issues can be viewed from a liberal or conservative point of view.

KEY TERMS

social problem	demography
status	survey research
role	sample
institution	cross-sectional data
social pathology	longitudinal data
social disorganization	participant observation
institution building	field research
conflict perspective	experimental group
secondary deviance	control group
ethnography	social policies

CHAPTER SUMMARY

What Is a Social Problem?

Social problems seem to be interrelated. Crime, poverty, lack of medical care, violence, drug abuse, and other behaviors rarely exist in isolation. These problems generate debates about causes and remedies; agreement that a problem exists does not imply consensus on a solution.

Social problems exist when enough people in a society agree that a condition exists that threatens their quality of life and core values, and that something must be done to remedy the situation. Social problems create controversies about the nature of the problem, its severity, and the best remedies. However, not all people count equally in defining social problems. Who defines social problems? Those with more power have greater influence in defining social problems.

Societal intervention, the idea that society should intervene to solve problems, is a recent one, developing in the late eighteenth century. The U.S. Constitution paved the way for this idea by providing individual guaranteed rights.

Perspectives on Social Problems

Some explanations of social problems seek to blame the individual and do not explain why the same pattern is repeated for entire groups of people. Sociological questions ask why a condition like homelessness exists, how it is distributed in society, and why some people are more at risk than others. **Table 1-1** outlines other social science approaches to the study of social problems, including history, cultural anthropology, psychology and social psychology, economics, and political science

So, the sociological perspective on social problems focuses on the social rather than individual aspects of a problem. Three major sociological perspectives: the functionalist, the conflict, and the interactionist, are powerful tools for understanding social problems. These perspectives are summarized in **Table 1-2**

Functionalists examine social ***institutions***, which are fairly stable structures of statuses and roles devoted to meeting the basic needs of people in a society. Basic assumptions include the following: we all hold positions in groups and organizations throughout our lives. These positions are referred to as ***statuses***, and have certain behavioral requirements called ***roles***. Statuses and roles are components of social institutions, which are stable structures that meet the basic needs of people in a society. Functionalists assume that roles have evolved to allow the social institution to fulfill its function in society. Hospitals, insurance companies, and private practices are organizations in this institution. Doctors, nurses, and patients are statuses in this institution. The focus for functionalists is on how social institutions operate.

Social problems are assumed to result from institutional failure to adapt to ongoing social change created by conditions such as wars, colonial conquest, disease and famine, population increases, and changing technologies of production. Change may produce disequilibrium as people no longer know how to perform roles and may turn to crime or develop mental illness.

All societies produce unique forms of crime and specific ways of responding to the crime. Those crimes that threaten the most cherished values are feared the most and produce the most severe punishment. Early functionalists saw social problems as a type of ***social pathology*** or illness that resulted when individuals or institutions failed to keep pace with changing conditions. Dissatisfaction with the subjectivity of this approach led functionalists to focus on social disorganization instead. The social pathology approach makes an organic analogy to physical disease.

Social disorganization theorists analyzed the consequences of immigration, urbanization, and industrialization. Social disorganization results when *normlessness, culture conflict*, and *breakdown* take place. Modern functionalists look at how institutions in society are organized to cope with new conditions.

After WWI, many groups that moved to cities were unable to adapt and ended up in crowded slums. Alcoholism, drug addiction, and crime rates rose drastically. Social disorganization theory developed to explain these patterns; the basic argument is that failed societal expectations produce normlessness, cultural conflict, and breakdown. Modern functionalism stresses the importance of ***institution-building***. This approach believes that social problems can be addressed by reforming social institutions.

The ***conflict perspective*** rejects the view that reforming social institutions will solve social problems. A basic belief is that social problems stem from major contradictions in the way society is constructed.

Marxist conflict theory assumes that social problems emerge from contradictions in the organization of capitalistic society; capitalism exploits workers because bosses are motivated by profit and not humanitarianism. The profit motive leads capitalists to search for ways to cut costs which threatens the livelihood of workers, who then may turn to crime or political rebellion. Thus, social problems are due to the ways that wealth and power become concentrated in the hands of a few people.

This approach stresses inequalities in the distribution of wealth and power; it is critical of attempts to reform social institutions. It is concerned with social movements that might change the basic structure of society. Marxist conflict theory cannot explain all kinds of conflict in society. Value conflict theorists stress the role of values in generating conflict and in understanding how powerful groups can impose their values on others.

Unlike functionalists, conflict theorists do not believe that reforming existing social institutions will eliminate social problems. This view is extended by ***value conflict*** theorists who believe that social problems result when groups with different values meet and compete. These theorists examine which groups hold which values and have the power to enforce them against the will of other groups.

There is a supposed broad conflict over deeply held values in the United States – some observers have called it a culture war between conservative and liberal political views.

The ***interactionist perspective*** shifts the level of analysis to the individual to look at processes whereby people become part of a situation defined as a social problem, and how people come to take on the values of the groups in which they participate. A key insight of this perspective stems from W. I. Thomas and colleagues' study of immigrants. Thomas found that some immigrants believed that bank robbery would be easier than work in factories. He concluded that the definition of the situation was central to understanding the actions of an individual or group. Mead and Cooley focused on the importance of interaction in peer groups in giving us our identity and our values.

Labeling theory, a variant of interactionism, sees the cause of a social problem as society's awareness that a specific behavior or problem exists and that it is defined as problematic. The labels attached to specific behaviors and people produce self-fulfilling prophecies because people tend to accept society's definitions and act accordingly.

This theory focuses on the impact of labels applied to those who deviate, and what this process says about society. Power differences result in inconsistency in labeling. The same act is not always seen as deviant. It depends on who does it. Social problems are seen as conditions that are defined as problematic by society. Those who are labeled deviant may engage in ***secondary deviance*** by adopting elements of a deviant lifestyle.

The interactionist perspective also contributes to what is known as the social construction approach to social problems, which contends that some claims about problems become dominant while others are ignored. This occurs because some claims are made by influential actors or opinion makers.

The Natural History of Social Problems

While the media may make social problems seem like fads, which come and go, sociologists have long recognized that social problems seem to develop in a series of stages. Spector and Kitsuse outlined the major stages that most social problems seem to go through. These are *problem definition, legitimacy, reemergence of demands, rejection, and institution building.*

The Media and Social Problems

The media, cable, Internet, TV magazine shows, and specialized magazines, have all shaped our perception of social problems. The speed of communication is one effect which can help avoid problems but can also spread fear. Sensationalism can mask important changes in social problems. **Figure 1-2** summarizes Americans' ranking in 2006 of major social problems.

Research on Social Problems

Sociologists conduct several types of research on social problems, including ethnography, demographic studies, survey research, field observation, and social experiments. ***Ethnography*** refers to the close observation of interactions among people in a social group or organization. The work of Newman and Wilson on fast-food jobs in the inner-city is an illustration of this method of doing research. Other examples are Duneier's research on the way people use public spaces and Erikson's research on the effects of a bank failure on migrant workers.

Demography is a subfield of sociology that studies how social conditions are distributed in human populations and how these populations are changing. Demographic studies typically seek to describe the incidence of a problem, which is then reported as an absolute number or a rate.

Surveys sample populations of people to learn about attitudes on issues like politics, unemployment, and crime, which is then aggregated and converted into numbers. Surveys can be ***cross-sectional*** (one point in time) or ***longitudinal*** (over some period of time). Surveys are a way of gathering information from a ***sample*** of people who represent the attitudes and behaviors of the population from which they were drawn. Surveys gather information by phone, mail, or in person that is aggregated and converted to numbers. The researcher must know who was interviewed, for what reason, and at what point in time.

Field research requires the researcher to participate directly in the lives of those being studied (***participant observation***) to understand the role of interaction in social problems. Neighborhoods, communities, and organizations are all examples of field settings. Becker's famous study of how people become drug users is an example of this type of work.

Social experiments systematically vary conditions to determine effects. Members of the ***experimental group*** receive a treatment that is not received by the ***control group***, but which is identical in all other ways. Results examine differences between these two conditions: if the treatment has an effect, then there will be a difference. If the treatment does not work, then there will be no difference between the control condition and the experimental condition.

Examples include the Wildcat experiment and the Zimbardo prison study. People who conduct research with human subjects must guarantee their rights of privacy, confidentiality, and informed consent.

Social Policy

Social policies are formal procedures designed to address social problems. They can be formulated by federal, state, and local government officials as well. Much research is designed to provide information for social policy decisions. Policy decisions are responsible for laws regulating banks, savings and loans, unemployment insurance, Social Security, and so on.

Going Beyond Left and Right

Conservatives and liberals have different views on social problems, with conservatives emphasizing the moral dimension and liberals emphasizing social conditions. Sociologists try to go beyond ideologies by looking at the consequences of different policies.

RESEARCH NAVIGATOR EXERCISES

(*NOTE: The number following articles cited is the Research Navigator I.D. # and may be used to access these articles)**

ContentSelect

Select the sociology database and enter the keyword *social problems*. Look for articles that relate to theoretical and methodological issues in the study of social problems. One example is a recent article surrounding a survey conducted by a national public policy group in Washington, D.C., suggesting that the learning environment in our nation's public schools is very poor. (AN 00287121, 1/18/2004)

New York Times Online

Select the sociology database, and enter the keyword *skin color*. Look for articles that deal with interracial prejudice. One illustration is an article entitled "New Jersey Policy Wins Praise for Efforts to End Profiling." (AN 1022103, 9/6/2007)

Link Library

Select the sociology database, and click on D. Next, select Demography and Migration, and then click on American Demographics. Look for articles that present demographic data. Next, click on U.S. Census Bureau. Look for the Special Topics section, and click on For Teachers. Next, select Reference Materials, and then select Fact Finder. Read the description of fact finding as done by the U.S. Census. What can be learned about social problems by looking at Census data?

PRACTICE TEST

MULTIPLE CHOICE QUESTIONS: Select the one best answer for each of the following questions.

1. Sociologists regard social problems as:
   a. conditions that seldom produce disagreement.
   b. a situation that exists when enough people define a situation as threatening to their quality of life and to cherished values.
   c. a matter of individual responsibility.
   d. existing only when social scientists have determined there is measurable empirical evidence that significant harm has been done to a society.

2. Women in the United States did not have the right to vote until:
   a. 1780.
   b. 1840.
   c. 1920.
   d. 1950.

3. Which of the following would be classified as a social problem by a sociologist?
   a. a couple who quarrel on their first date
   b. a woman who just lost her first job
   c. homeless women
   d. a man who feels stressed and overworked

4. A status refers to a:
   a. position in an organization or group.
   b. structure that is devoted to meeting basic needs for society.
   c. set of expected behaviors.
   d. none of the above

5. Which of the following is NOT of interest to the functionalist?
   a. how the role of the nurse helps the health-care system to function
   b. how the change from agricultural production to industrial production changed the roles of mothers and fathers
   c. how the rich are able to determine what kinds of behaviors are seen as social problems
   d. why particular crimes are committed and punished in some societies, but not in others

6. The social pathology perspective:
   a. represents a recent trend in functionalism that is seen as useful.
   b. sees social problems as a form of illness in society.
   c. focuses on how people come to be labeled as ill.
   d. stems from Marx's work on class conflict.

7. Social disorganization is manifested in three major ways. These are:
   a. normlessness, class conflict, and breakdown.
   b. class conflict, culture conflict, and breakdown.
   c. normlessness, culture conflict, and breakdown.
   d. normlessness, culture conflict, and class conflict.

8. According to social disorganization theorists, when blacks perform well in school but encounter job discrimination, their frustration may lead to:
   a. normlessness.
   b. class conflict.
   c. culture conflict.
   d. breakdown.

9. Marxist conflict theorists assume that:
   a. workers are exploited by their bosses, who own the means of production.
   b. social problems can be traced to inequalities in wealth and power which engender many forms of conflict.
   c. displaced workers may turn to crime to overturn the capitalist system.
   d. all of the above

10. Marxist conflict theorists:
   a. want to reform existing institutions.
   b. conduct research on social movements among the poor that might change the way society is organized.
   c. assume that social organizations and institutions do not function as intended.
   d. believe that it is the lifestyle of the poor that causes social problems.

11. The _____ theorist believes that deviance from society's rules results from the fact that some groups disagree with those rules and feel free to break them if they can.
   a. value conflict
   b. Marxist conflict
   c. exchange
   d. behaviorist

12. The _____ perspective looks at the process by which people take on the values of the groups to which they belong.
   a. functionalist
   b. conflict
   c. interactionist
   d. none of the above

13. ________ stated that situations people define as real are real in their consequences.
   a. W. I. Thomas
   b. G. H. Mead
   c. H. Cooley
   d. David Klein

14. According to labeling theory, the way to solve social problems is to:
   a. increase the severity of the punishment.
   b. change the definition for what is considered deviant.
   c. increase media awareness of a problem.
   d. change the class structure.

15. The _______ approach argues that some claims about social problems become dominant while others remain weak.
   a. secondary deviance
   b. labeling
   c. social construction
   d. none of the above

16. According to Spector and Kitsuse, social problems seem to go through a series of stages. Identify the correct order of these stages.
   a. rejection and institution building, problem definition, legitimacy, reemergence of demands
   b. problem definition, legitimacy, reemergence of demands, rejection and institution building
   c. legitimacy, problem definition, rejection and institution building, reemergence of demands
   d. rejection and institution building, problem definition, legitimacy, reemergence of demands

17. A study that reports the rate of child abuse in the United States is most likely a/an _______study.
   a. demographic
   b. experiment
   c. ethnography
   d. field

18. A/an ______ is a number of people who represent the behavior and attitudes of the larger population from which it was drawn.
   a. experiment
   b. subset
   c. sample
   d. population

19. Howard Becker's classic study of marijuana smokers highlighted:
   a. the adverse effects of marijuana.
   b. how definitions of the situation shaped perception of the experience.
   c. the fact that most smokers responded exactly the same way.
   d. none of the above

20. In an experiment, the ______ group receives a treatment, while the _____ group does not.
   a. control, experimental
   b. experimental, control
   c. pseudo-experimental, control
   d. field, experimental

ESSAY QUESTIONS

1. Provide an example of a "contradiction" that has been created through globalization.

2. Explain the sociological perspective on social problems and provide one or two examples of the importance of this view.

3. Compare and contrast the three major theoretical perspectives on social problems.

4. Your text discusses other approaches to the study of social problems. Provide a brief overview of the way that historians, cultural anthropologists, psychologists, economists, and political scientists approach social problems.

5. Differentiate between the Marxist and value conflict perspectives on social problems.

6. Compare and contrast the major research methods used to investigate social problems.

7. Compare and contrast the conservative and liberal perspectives on social policies.

8. Explain the natural history approach to social problems and identify the stages that Spector and Kitsuse described.

ANSWERS TO MULTIPLE CHOICE QUESTIONS

1.	b	11.	a
2.	c	12.	c
3.	c	13.	a
4.	a	14.	b
5.	c	15.	c
6.	b	16.	b
7.	c	17.	a
8.	d	18.	c
9.	d	19.	b
10.	b	20.	b

CHAPTER TWO

Problems of Health and Health Care

CHAPTER OUTLINE

I. Health Care as a Global Social Problem
II. The Scope of Health-Care Problems in America
  A. Unequal Access to Health Care
    1. Inequalities of Race and Ethnicity
    2. Inequalities of Social Class
    3. Inequalities of Gender
  B. The High Cost of Health Care
    1. Hospitals
    2. Physicians
    3. Medical Technologies
    4. Prescription Drugs
    5. Demographic and Cultural Factors
    6. Obesity
    7. Smoking
    8. Risky Behaviors and Costly Procedures
    9. Unequal Access
  C. Inadequate Protection
    1. The Uninsured
    2. Cost Shifting
  D. Women and Health Care
  E. The Disabled and Handicapped
  F. Ethical Issues
    1. End-of-Life and Advanced Directives
    2. Privacy and Patients' Rights
III. AIDS—A Modern Plague
  A. AIDS and Global Poverty
  B. AIDS Orphans
IV. Explanations of Health-Care Problems
  A. Class and Class Conflict
  B. Institutions and Health Care
  C. Health and Social Interaction
V. Social Policy
  A. Managed Care
  D. Insurance Reform
  E. Working, but without Health Care
  F. The Disabled and Handicapped
  G. Social Policy and AIDS
  H. Future Prospects
VI. Going Beyond Left and the Right
VII. Summary
VIII. Key Terms
IX. Social Problems Online
X. Research Navigator

LEARNING OBJECTIVES

After reading Chapter Two you should:

1. Be familiar with health care as a global social problem; be aware of the problems faced by developed as well as developing nations.
2. Be able to define medical sociology and explain how medical sociologists analyze health-care issues.
3. Understand the factors that influence the cost of health care in the United States.
4. Be familiar with the different types of insurance in the United States and which groups of people are most likely to have each type.
5. Be familiar with the problems associated with Medicare and Medicaid.
6. Be familiar with how race, class, and gender impact the quality of health care.
7. Be able to apply each of the major theoretical perspectives to the analysis of health care.
8. Be able to discuss research on AIDS, and be familiar with AIDS as a global health problem.
9. Be familiar with issues of legislation as they impact the disabled and the handicapped.
10. Be familiar with social policies dealing with health care reform, managed care, and HMOs.

KEY TERMS

obesity
health maintenance organization (HMO)
cost shifting
managed care

CHAPTER SUMMARY

Health Care as a Global Social Problem

Health care presents a variety of social problems to all the world's societies. The United Nations rates nations on the basis of a series of indicators of health, education, equality of political participation, and many other factors. The nations are then grouped into high, medium, and low levels of human development for purpose of comparison. Affluent countries face problems with equal access while impoverished countries must deal with infectious diseases, high infant/maternal mortality rates, low life expectancies, scarce medical personnel, and inadequate water/sewer systems. **Table 2-1** shows how much or little improvement various nations have made in two key health indicators: life expectancy and infant mortality.

Medical sociology is the subfield of sociology that studies the health-care system and its impact on the public, especially access to health care. Sociologists want to know how social characteristics like social class affect access to health care; they also see health-care institutions as a source of difficulty.

The Scope of Health-Care Problems in America

The range of situations in which health care is a social problem is wide and exists at a micro and macro level. Issues to consider include unequal access to health services, the high cost of health services, the high cost of health care, inadequate insurance coverage, special issues faced by women and the handicapped, and ethical issues linked to medical technology.

Health care is distributed very unevenly in the United States. Over 18 percent of Americans under the age of 65 have no health insurance. Access to care is shaped by race, class, and gender. Nonwhites, the poor, and women are adversely affected by lack of access to high-quality health care: each of these groups experiences more health problems due to a lack of insurance and poverty.

Life expectancy differs for whites and nonwhites as does infant mortality. Even when income is the same, nonwhites have higher death and illness rates and tend to receive less care than whites for heart disease, asthma, breast cancer, HIV infection, and nursing home care. Race affects the likelihood of being placed in intensive care and of receiving procedures like cardiac catheterization.

There is a strong relationship between class and illness; lower-class members are sick more often, more likely to be disabled, and to have higher mortality rates. Low income affects health from birth. Poor newborns have a higher mortality rate due to low birth weight, poor maternal diet and drug use, and lack of prenatal care. Medicaid was enacted in 1965 and has served more than 30 million people. The 1996 Medicaid reform reduced medical care funding, with the result that many poor people receive less medical care.

Women are also less likely to get adequate health care in the United States. Kaiser Family Foundation found that more women than men skipped or delayed needed medical treatment or could not fill prescriptions. About 30 percent of low-income women lack health insurance; nearly 60 percent of women without health insurance worked full time or part time.

Unequal access is related to the cost of obtaining it. High costs are related to declining personal income, dwindling government resources, hospital-based care, new drugs and technologies, risky behaviors, and increased physician specialization. Much of the increase is due to increases in the cost of prescription drugs; however, cultural factors related to lifestyle, such as obesity, smoking, bad diet, sedentary lifestyle, and risky behaviors, are also factors.

Medical technologies like angioplasty, renal dialysis, sonograms, CAT scans, MRIs, and organ transplantation have all increased the cost of health care.

Increased costs have led to a tendency to shift costs to the public and to churn insurance policies so as to avoid liability for risky patients. Health-care expenditures have increased from $1,002 per capita in 1980 to $5,804 in 2002. The United States has seen the highest increases among highly developed countries, as shown in **Figure 2.2**.

In 2003, United States health-care costs amounted to 15 percent of the GDP.

Hospital costs rose at a dramatic pace until the 1990s. Cost increases have slowed somewhat due to preadmission testing in outpatient departments, reduced hospital stays, and more procedures being moved to outpatient settings. Such measures have a disproportionate impact on the poor and elderly.

The cost of physicians' services has increased.

Medical technologies are another reason for high medical costs.

The cost of prescription drugs is a major factor in the high cost of health care, accounting for about 45 percent of the annual increase in U.S. health-care costs.

Demographic and cultural factors are also at work; the population is aging but is also living longer. Lifestyle issues like smoking, drinking, diet, high stress, and sedentary lifestyle increase costs.

Obesity is increasingly a problem; 60 percent of Americans are overweight; 26 percent are obese; 6 million are "super-obese," meaning that they are more than 100 pounds overweight. Obesity accounts for 280,000 deaths per year.

Smoking is the leading preventable cause of death with 430,000 deaths per year. A total of 3,000 young people become regular tobacco users every day, and one-third will eventually die from smoking-related causes.

Risky behaviors and costly procedures are also involved. Sports injuries and up-to-date treatments also drive up health-care costs.

Unequal access also plays a role, as diseases that could be prevented are not. **Table 2-3** shows the potential cost savings from early preventive medicine of social services for different health issues.

For much of the nation's history, individuals paid for their own health care and insurance. This meant that poor people received care only in extreme emergencies. In the 1930s, we began to develop a system in which costs were shared by employers, individuals, and the government. There are now three categories of health insurance: ***HMOs,*** or ***health maintenance organizations*** that are prepaid groups, commercial insurance companies like Blue Cross and Blue Shield that sell both individual and group policies, and public insurance (Medicaid and Medicare).

Public health insurance like Medicaid and Medicare help the poor and elderly, but many millions have no coverage at all because they do not earn enough to pay for it despite working full time. While Medicare is designed to cover health-care costs for the elderly, it does not cover the cost of prescriptions or nursing home care. Medicaid only covers costs for the very poor. Medicare and Medicaid are expensive and are subject to many rules, making them unappealing to many doctors. Also, Medicare does not cover the costs of nursing homes.

There are more than 45 million uninsured in the United States. Sixty percent of these are 18-to-64 year-olds who worked full time. **Figure 2-5** shows household income and the employment status of the uninsured. The very poor who don't work get Medicaid, and the elderly get Medicare. Most other people receive health insurance from an employer; they may make contributions as well. Smaller firms are less likely to do this. Minority status increases the chances of being uninsured.

Cost shifting, the tendency for the costs of treating people with serious illnesses to be transferred from one insurance system to another, is a major problem; $10 billion per year is passed on to the public. Policy churning is often practiced by insurance companies to raise rates for high-risk patients.

Women's issues include the controversy over legalized abortion, the role of midwives in the birth process, as well as the need for more monies to fund research on women's health issues. Abortion rights won in *Roe v. Wade* have come under attack.

Hospitals restrict activities of midwives; doctors retain controls over the birth process. Anesthesia, induced labor, and surgical practices such as Caesarian section and the use of forceps have come under attack. Lack of funding for medical problems is also a problem for women, as the National Institutes of Health spends only 20 percent of its budget on women's health issues, even though 40,000 women die each year from breast cancer.

Like women, the disabled and handicapped have encountered problems of access. They are likely to be unemployed and have high poverty rates. Several key pieces of legislation including the ADA have been enacted, making it illegal to discriminate against the disabled. The cost of physician services has increased in the twentieth century due to a shortage of physicians, clustering in the metropolitan areas, increased specialization, and rising medical malpractice insurance.

The disabled suffer from extremely high unemployment rates and underemployment. Yet, disabled workers have only a slightly higher than average absenteeism rate, and turnover is low. Approximately 32 million Americans have deformities or other impairments; another 33 million have visual/auditory impairments. They have emerged as a recognized minority group.

New technologies can prolong life but are costly and raise ethical questions of who receives them. Assisted suicides have become an issue and advanced directives have become more common. The Terri Schiavo case called attention to the controversy over the problem of death with dignity in a situation in which a patient is on life support but has left no clear "advance directives." Another major medical-ethical issue concerns patients' right to privacy and control over their medical records.

AIDS: A Modern Plague

The AIDS epidemic presents many health-care problems. First identified in the 1980s, HIV has a long period of latency. AIDS drugs are available mainly in affluent nations; it is a global epidemic. WHO estimates that more than 40 million are HIV positive, and 85 percent of these cases are in developing nations of sub-Saharan Africa and Asia.

HIV is transmitted via bodily fluids (blood, semen, or vaginal secretions). Approximately 30 percent of the new cases in the United States are found among women. To date in the United States at least 524,000 people have died of AIDS. Death rates are declining due to new treatments and safer sex practices.

Poverty plays a major role in the spread of HIV, particularly among women. In impoverished regions of southern Africa, high rates of HIV transmission are often found among the most mobile populations.

Researchers at the World AIDS Conference say there are 15 million AIDS orphans; these children may have to drop out of school to care for their dying parents and orphaned siblings. There is no cure for AIDS, and the drugs used to treat it are expensive and strains the health-care system. AIDS can be viewed as three epidemics rolled into one: the spread of HIV, AIDS, and reactions to the disease. Treatment for AIDS is extremely expensive; as there is no cure, behavioral changes are the best defense against further spread.

Explanations of Health-Care Problems

The three major theoretical perspectives offer different explanations for health-care problems. Conflict theorists stress the role that capitalism and pursuit of profit play in creating problems of access. Recent trends suggest that less profitable patients may not receive treatment. Functionalists, who are opposed to treating health care as a commodity, examine features of health-care institutions to see how they might be changed to improve the situation. Interactionists focus on lifestyle issues and patterns of sociability.

Social class goes a long way toward explaining the types of illness experienced by members of a household. The poor are more likely to be weak due to inadequate diet and are exposed to unhealthy environmental conditions. The trend away from public hospitals toward for-profit hospitals may mean avoiding treatment for less profitable patients.

Functionalists stress the features of the health-care institutions themselves, and believe that health care should not be treated as a commodity. The reasons for this include inaccessible information for the patient, product uncertainty, norms of treatment, lack of price competition, restricted entry, professional dominance, and misallocated supply.

The poor health of Americans is due in part to our lifestyles, sedentary occupations, bad diet, lack of exercise, pollution, and cigarette smoking. Interactionists believe that patterns of sociability are important in shaping these patterns. The most pervasive problems stem from smoking. Approximately 45 million people continue to smoke; more than 1,100 deaths per day and a greater number of serious illnesses are attributable to smoking. Research shows that magazines with high revenues from cigarette companies are less likely to publicize the dangers of smoking.

Social Policy

American health care is in crisis. Too many households lack medical insurance, the costs of medical goods/services is mounting, malpractice insurance is rising, and the cost of insurance is rising. Health care is a problem for all industrialized nations, but the United States lags behind the others. Canada has a national health-care system that provides the same care to all, but it has less advanced technologies and has contributed to higher taxes.

The United States has been moving toward ***managed care*** that limits access to medical care. The rise of managed care has tended to limit patients' ability to freely choose their doctors, because patients in most plans, and especially HMOs, receive full coverage for services only if they choose a physician within the plan's network.

Physicians and patients agree that managed care is leading to a reduction in the quality of health care. Medicare costs have begun to rise again after a brief period of decline between the 1980s and 1990s. Prescription drug costs and the recession are partly to blame. In 2002, Congress failed to pass a prescription drug bill. In 2003, at the urging of the Bush administration, Congress passed legislation to extend coverage for some prescription drugs for people over age 65 who are covered under Medicare. In the 2006 congressional elections, Democrats promised to revise the prescription drug law.

The current crisis in the U.S. medical care system is significantly worsened by a large-scale retreat from employer-provided health insurance.

The Rehabilitation Act of 1973 prohibited government agencies and contractors from discriminating against the handicapped. In 1977, the Department of Health and Human Services (HHS) began to require all recipients of HHS funds to provide equal access to employment and services. These rulings meant that new buildings must have ramps and elevators. The Education for All Handicapped Children Act of 1975 gave the right to a free appropriate public education. The ADA (Americans with Disabilities Act) passed in 1990, bars discrimination against the disabled in employment, transportation, public accommodation, and telecommunications.

New costly treatments raise difficult policy issues. More babies will be born with AIDS; therefore, educational programs directed at young women and adolescents are important. The World Health Organization (WHO) stresses the need to prevent HIV infection in women and to reduce the impact of HIV on women. Other policy issues include how to prevent AIDS among IV drug users and how to speed up discovery and manufacture of new drugs.

As the 2008 presidential election approaches, health-care reform is once again a major campaign issue. It remains to be seen whether the American electorate will send a determined enough message to its political leadership to institute universal health-care coverage.

Going Beyond Left and Right

Almost every major health initiative—end-of-life measures, research on stem cells, funding for women's reproductive health, funding for safe sex practices, and the reform of health-care systems, either in the United States or globally - is fraught with issues that originate in deep ideological divisions and moral dilemmas. Health-care policy in the United States will continue to move in small but important steps, avoiding major ideological confrontations.

RESEARCH NAVIGATOR EXERCISES

ContentSelect

Select the nursing, health, and medicine database. Use the keywords *poverty* and *health* to look for research on the link between poverty and health. An example of this is "Mental Health and Poverty in Developing Nations: Revisiting the Relationship" (*AN 25624139*, August, 2007). What IS the relationship? Try to integrate the concepts presented in your textbook in evaluating this article.

New York Times Online

Use sociology as the subject, and use the keywords *minorities* and *health care*. Look for the article "Aging and Gay, and Facing Prejudice in Twilight" (Oct 9, 2007). After you have read the article, evaluate the relationship between the social implications of aging, health, being homosexual in a largely heterosexual world, and the challenges of prejudice and discrimination.

Link Library

Use sociology as the subject. Click on H for health care. Click on the Economics of Health Care Quiz to test your knowledge of the health-care industry in the United States. How did you do? Where and how do you learn about how the health-care industry works in the United States?

PRACTICE TEST

MULTIPLE CHOICE QUESTIONS: Select the one best answer for each of the following questions.

1. Differences in life expectancy between developed and less developed countries are due largely to:
   a. the number of doctors in the country.
   b. a decline in breast-feeding.
   c. the chance that people survive childhood diseases and parasites.
   d. contaminated food and water supplies.

2. ________ is the subfield of sociology that specializes in research on the health-care system and its impact on the public.
   a. Medical sociology
   b. Epidemiology
   c. Gerontology
   d. Oncology

3. Health care is distributed very unevenly in the United States. Today, approximately ____ percent of Americans under age 65 do not currently have any health insurance, and millions more have inadequate coverage.
   a. 18
   b. 9
   c. 28
   d. 41

4. Even with equivalent insurance, racial and ethnic minorities are likely to receive less or inferior care compared with whites for which of the following conditions?
   a. heart disease
   b. asthma
   c. HIV infection
   d. all of the above

5. A study of 18,000 male civil service employees found that mortality rates varied directly with the individuals' _______.
   a. race
   b. gender
   c. job classification
   d. region of country

6. Expenditures on health care in the United States in 2002 amounted to $ _____ per capita.
   a. $945
   b. $1,534
   c. $3,672
   d. $5,804

7. In 2003, spending on health care in the United States amounted to about 15 percent of the GDP. Which of the following countries spent the highest proportions of their respective GDPs on health care?
   a. Sweden
   b. the U.S.
   c. Canada
   d. France

8. Which of the following have been factors that caused an increase in the cost of physician services?
   a. a shortage of physicians
   b. specialization
   c. malpractice insurance
   d. all of the above

9. The Centers for Disease Control estimates that about ____ Americans die each year as a direct consequence of obesity.
   a. 2,800   c. 280,000
   b. 28,000   d. 2,800,000

10. Data from the CDC indicate that more than ______ deaths per year are attributed to tobacco use.
   a. 4,300   c. 330,000
   b. 30,400   d. 430,000

11. Which program is paid for with Social Security taxes and is intended to cover some of the medical expenses of those over 65?
   a. Medicare
   b. Medicaid
   c. Health Maintenance Organization
   d. Temporary Aid for Needy Families

12. ________refers to transferring the cost of treating people with serious illnesses from one insurance system to another.
   a. Benefit shifting
   b. Policy shifting
   c. Cost shifting
   d. Cost reassignment

13. Which of the following is true of lay midwives who practice outside of medical control?
   a. They can legally practice in all states.
   b. They are not fully legal in all states.
   c. They are not legal in any state.
   d. They are not present throughout the entire childbirth process.

14. Which of the following are true of the disabled?
   a. They suffer from high unemployment rates.
   b. Many are underemployed.
   c. They have below average turnover rates.
   d. All of the above are true.

15. Which of the following is NOT true of AIDS?
   a. It is caused by HIV.
   b. There is a brief period of latency.
   c. It attacks the body's immune system.
   d. Anti-AIDS drugs have been effective in preventing the onset of AIDS symptoms.

16. The World Health Organization estimates that more than ____ people are infected with HIV.
   a. 400 million   c. 4 million
   b. 40 million   d. 1 million

17. In the United States, at least _______ people have died of AIDS since 1981.
   a. 4,300   c. 524,000
   b. 40,080   d. 2,400,100

18. According to the text, the functionalist perspective argues that medical care should not be treated as a commodity because of which of the following?
    a. restricted entry
    b. lack of price competition
    c. norms of treatment
    d. all of the above

19. According to the text, which of the following are among the health problems related to the patterns of sociability in the United States?
    a. excessive eating
    b. alcohol consumption
    c. smoking
    d. all of the above

20. The _______ Act bars discrimination against the disabled in employment, transportation, public accommodations, and telecommunications.
    a. Rehabilitation
    b. Education for all Handicapped Children
    c. Americans with Disabilities
    d. No Child Left Behind

ESSAY QUESTIONS

1. Explain why health care is a global social problem. Be sure to explain how health care varies with the degree of human development.

2. Describe the scope of health-care problems in the United States.

3. How does race and ethnicity impact health care in the United States?

4. Explain the factors that increase the cost of health care in the United States.

5. Discuss the problems associated with the spread of AIDS throughout the world.

6. Compare/contrast the functionalist, conflict, and interactionist perspectives on health-care problems.

ANSWERS TO MULTIPLE CHOICE QUESTIONS

1.	c	11.	a
2.	a	12.	c
3.	a	13.	b
4.	d	14.	d
5.	c	15.	d
6.	d	16.	b
7.	b	17.	c
8.	d	18.	d
9.	c	19.	d
10.	d	20.	c

CHAPTER THREE

Problems of Mental Illness and Treatments

CHAPTER OUTLINE

I. Mental Illness as a Social Problem
   A. Perspectives on Mental Illness
   B. Suicide and Mental Illness
II. The Social Construction of Mental Illness
   A. Defining Mental Illness
      1. The Medical Model
      2. Mental Illness as Deviance
      3. Problems in Living
   B. Classification of Mental Disorders
   C. Diagnosis or Label?
      1. Mental Illness Among Combatants in Afghanistan and Iraq
III. Inequality, Conflict, and Mental Illness
   A. Incidence versus Prevalence of Mental Disorders
   B. Social Class and Mental Disorder
      1. The Drift Hypothesis
   C. Mental Disorder and Urban Life
   D. Other Factors
      1. Race
      2. Sex
      3. Age
IV. Institutional Problems of Treatment and Care
   A. Methods of Treatment
      1. Nonmedical Forms of Treatment
      2. Medical Approaches to Treatment
   B. Changes in Mental Health Treatment and Care
   C. Treatment Institutions
      1. Mental Hospitals
      2. Community Psychology
      3. Cost Shifting and the Two-Class Mental-Health System
   D. Deinstitutionalization and Homelessness
V. Social Policy
   A. Future Prospects
VI. Going Beyond Left and Right
VII. Summary
VIII. Key Terms
IX. Social Problems Online
X. Research Navigator

LEARNING OBJECTIVES

After reading Chapter Three you should:

1. Be able to distinguish between mental illness and mental disorder.
2. Be familiar with the extent of mental illness in the United States, and which problems are most common.
3. Be aware of the problem of deinstitutionalization.
4. Be familiar with suicide as a social problem and know about the incidence of this problem.
5. Understand how interactionists, functionalists, and conflict theorists approach the analysis of mental illness.
6. Know what is meant by the "medical model" as applied to mental disorders.
7. Know what is meant by residual deviance, and how it might play a role in creating mental illness.
8. Know how mental illnesses are classified by the American Psychiatric Association, and how the DSM classifications may affect treatment.
9. Know how diagnoses can sometimes arbitrarily label people and what consequences may ensue from those labels.
10. Understand the impact of inequality on the incidence and treatment of mental illness.
11. Understand the relationship between social class and mental disorder.
12. Be able to describe and explain the drift hypothesis.
13. Be familiar with the research on crowding and mental disorder.
14. Be familiar with research on race and sex and their relationship to mental disorder.
15. Know about the methods of treatment of mental illness, including medical and nonmedical approaches.
16. Be familiar with the settings in which treatments are typically carried out, including mental hospitals and halfway houses.
17. Know what is meant by cost shifting in the mental-health system.
18. Know how deinstitutionalization and homelessness are related.
19. Be familiar with the social policy debates on mental illness, especially mental-health insurance needs.
20. Understand the relationship between attention deficits, eating disorders, and social policy.

KEY TERMS

mental disorder
mental illness
deinstitutionalization
residual deviance
social-selection (drift) hypothesis
psychotropic drugs
total institution
community psychology
halfway house

CHAPTER SUMMARY

Mental Illness as a Social Problem

Mental disorder and ***mental illness*** are terms that are often used interchangeably. However, the form refers to mental problems that require hospitalization or close medical supervision. Until the 20th century, many people with physical ailments were mistakenly placed in mental hospitals. Around the world, mental illness is a "profoundly underestimated" social problem. Approximately 80 percent of the world's 450 million mentally disabled people live in developing nations.

While mental illness may have both biological and social causes, it is important to realize that whatever the cause, mental illness is a social problem because of the number of people affected, and because of the strain placed on social institutions.

The mental disorders that cause severe social problems are those associated with extreme forms of mental illness, such as sociopaths. However, social problems are also created by mentally ill who are less threatening to public safety, but who nevertheless create social strains and costs.

In the United States, panic attacks and phobias are the most common forms of mental problems. Phobias include severe fears such as fear of going outside, fear of heights, or fear of being in an enclosed space. Phobias and panic attacks affect an estimated 20 million Americans in any given year. Another 18 million suffer from depression.

As **Table 3-1** reveals, three of the top ten causes of role impairment days are mental disorders, not physical ones. A distressing aspect of the problem of mental illness is the social impact of ***deinstitutionalization***, or discharging patients from mental hospitals directly into the community.

Policy makers look to sociologists and other social scientists for basic research on the causes of mental illness and the impact of policies initiatives to recommend how to deal with trends in mental illness.

Mental illness, or mental disorder, is a social problem that has been studied by interactionists, conflict theorists, and functionalists. Interactionists examine the impact of labels, which they believe may lead some to actually behave in ways that are consistent with the label. Conflict theorists focus on the association of mental illness with deprivation and inequality. For example, they see a link between social class and mental illness and the emergence of two-class mental-health care. Typically, more affluent patients have access to higher-quality care than less affluent patients. Functionalists look more at how mental illnesses challenge our ability to treat them.

Suicide rates have steadily increased since 1950. Worldwide, suicide accounts for 2 percent of all deaths. Mental illness seems to account for a great deal (but not all) of suicide. Some suicides may have biological causes; others result from rational choices, such as suicides to avoid embarrassment or suffering. In the young, however, suicide is almost always the result of depression or other forms of mental illness.

The Social Construction of Mental Illness

Some sociologists have looked at the social construction of mental illness to describe how different groups define mental illness. Three ways of defining mental illness are the medical model, which views mental illness as a disease; the deviance approach, which looks at how society and the individual react to being labeled mentally ill; and the view that mental illness is a diagnosis used to control social, ethical, or legal deviations.

The medical model views mental disorders as a disease with a biological cause that primarily is remedied by treating the patient. Biological sciences have uncovered strong evidence to support biological explanations of mental disorders like schizophrenia. Other mental disorders appear at birth, like Down syndrome, which present unusual and difficult challenges to those afflicted by them.

The medical model led to serious investigation of the causes and cures of mental illness, as opposed to older notions that those afflicted were mad or possessed. This has led to modern therapies and has reduced the stigma associated with mental disorders.

Disadvantages of the medical model include disregard for the wider social environment as a possible source for mental disorders. Hospitalized individuals may recover, but may still be unable to cope when they return to outer tensions. Additionally, mental illnesses that have physiological causes may be worsened by an individual's social environment.

Social scientists who take the view of mental illness as deviance see that the way people are treated once they have been diagnosed with a mental disorder can have a lasting impact on their behavior and on chances of leading a happy and productive life. When society decides to label behavior that violates social conventions as mental illness, an individual labeled as such may accept that role and comply with the expectations of that role. Thus, a disorder may not only be a function of an individual's inability to comply with social expectations but also a function of the label attached to the individual who deviates. ***Residual deviance*** refers to violation of social conventions that are so completely taken for granted that they seem like human nature.

Thomas Szasz argues that problems in living are mislabeled as mental illness; doing so allows doctors to treat social, ethical, or legal deviations as illnesses, which become an issue of justice and individual freedom. For example, shabby and dirty people whose bizarre behavior is interpreted as mental illness can by involuntarily placed in shelters or hospitals.

Classifications of mental illness have been created and refined by the American Psychiatric Association. The American Psychiatric Association has created the *Diagnostic and Statistical Manual of Mental Disorders*, which classifies mental disorders, but which is also based on the medical model of mental illness. Recent editions have addressed some of the more controversial issues. **Table 3-2** provides a list of the categories of mental disorders listed in the DSM-IV.

These classifications have helped create a common language that has helped therapists develop consistent treatment plans. Clinicians and researchers need a common language to discuss mental disorders. It is impossible to plan a consistent program of treatment for a patient without an accurate diagnosis, and it is impossible to evaluate the effectiveness of various forms of treatment without clearly defined diagnostic terms. Some have argued that these classifications are arbitrary and have contributed to the problems associated with labeling people as mentally ill.

There are three problems with labeling people as mentally ill: 1) it makes us perceive certain behaviors as sick; 2) it gives public agencies the right to incarcerate people against their will simply for not conforming; and 3) it causes those people to define themselves as rule breakers and undesirables and allows them to fulfill that image. However, recent studies have shown that interviewers with basic training in the diagnosis of mental illness can spot people with serious mental disorders.

The treatment of soldiers with PTSD may improve as a result of a recent, highly publicized study of the mental-health needs of soldiers returning from Afghanistan and Iraq. In 2007, a special report to the U.S. military by the American Psychological Association revealed that the military's mental-health system is overwhelmed and understaffed, with almost 40 percent of mental-health positions in military hospitals and bases unfilled.

Inequality, Conflict, and Mental Illness

Sociologists are interested in the relationship between social factors, like poverty, and the incidence of mental disorders, and have studied such factors as poverty, the effects of urban life, and the impact of race and sex. Although statistics on mental disorders are only rough estimates, sociologists have reached several tentative conclusions about the relationship. Conflict theorists call attention to the ways in which inequalities of wealth and power produce inequalities in access to effective treatment. Additionally, poverty itself can create stress that leads to mental illness.

Although not in perfect agreement, studies since the 1930s have shown a relationship between social class and mental disorder. Most of these studies suggest that mental illness is more common among the lowest socioeconomic class. Because of different data-collection techniques and different definitions of mental illness, estimates of the proportion of mentally ill vary. Epidemiological studies of mental illness are costly and cannot be conducted every year, but they do provide a baseline on which social policy is based.

The ***social selection*** or ***drift hypothesis*** suggests that social class is not the cause of mental illness; rather it argues that people drift to the lower classes because their illness prevents them from functioning at the higher classes. **Figure 3-1** illustrates the vicious cycle of poverty and mental illness.

There has been little research in the relationship between mental disorder and urban life; research is difficult because most mental hospitals are in urban areas, which tends to concentrate mental disorders there. Some studies suggest that mental illness is associated with overcrowding in the home, although others have criticized these studies.

Other factors that potentially influence mental illness, such as race and sex, have been investigated. Race does not appear to be a significant variable by itself. Relationships with race are more likely to be explained by relationships between race and social class: blacks and Hispanics are more likely to be poor.

Overall rates of mental illness are about the same for men and women, although women are more likely than men to suffer from depression, anxieties, and phobias. Some of these differences could be explained by different gender-based expectations for mental health that conform to traditional sex roles. The question of whether men and women have different rates of psychosis has not been resolved.

Age is also a factor. In contrast to most severe disabling physical diseases, mental illness begins early in life. Mental disorders can be thought of as the chronic disorders of the young. Fifty percent of all lifetime cases of mental disorders worldwide begin by age 14. Three-quarters have begun by age 24.

Institutional Problems of Treatment and Care

The treatment of mental disorders has made a great deal of progress in the last century, but has many problems, especially in creating and maintaining effective institutions for the treatment and care of the mentally ill. The hospitalization of the mentally ill has given way to community-based treatments that attempt to help the mentally ill cope with their environments. This is, in part, due to advances in psychotropic drugs, but also to fiscal pressures to find more economical treatments. This deinstitutionalization of the mentally ill may be contributing to higher rates of mental illness among the homeless.

The two major approaches to the treatment of mental disorders are psychotherapy and medical treatment in the form of ***psychotropic drugs*** (drugs used to treat mental illness) or electroconvulsive therapy. Sometimes these forms are used simultaneously, but they involve different groups of mental health professionals.

Patients who undergo psychotherapy are helped to understand the underlying reasons for their problems so that they can try to work out solutions. The process involves some form of interaction between the patient and the therapist or among patients in groups. Among the major forms or psychotherapy are psychoanalysis, client-centered therapy, and various types of therapy and support groups. Hypnosis is another form of nonmedical treatment.

Medical treatments, particularly chemotherapy and shock treatment, are applied to the most severe mental illness. Control over these treatments is in the hands of medical or clinical psychiatrists.

Shock therapy was used extensively in the 1940s and early 1950s, but as drug therapies were developed it fell into disfavor. Recently, interest has been revived as drug therapies have turned out to be less effective than anticipated.

Developments in drug therapies have helped patients deal with the incapacitating effects of their illnesses, but they have side effects when used over long periods of time. It is generally believed that chemotherapy should be used in conjunction with some other form of therapy, since drugs alone can rarely bring about significant long-term changes in behavior.

Surveys of mental health needs indicate that large proportions of mentally ill go untreated. To effectively address the needs of people with mental disorders, a variety of institutions and approaches are required. Schools, hospitals, families, community centers, and law enforcement agencies need to become more aware of mental-health problems and how to deal with them. Failure to overcome stigma, discrimination, and lack of support, as well as funding, must be addressed to effectively cope with mental disorders. **Figure 3-2** illustrates the needs of people with mental disorders.

Psychotherapy and other non-medical forms of treatment generally occur in nonhospital settings, but medical treatments often require hospitalization. This section looks at treatment in institutional settings.

In the late nineteenth and early twentieth centuries, mental hospitals were built in secluded spots, not only to protect patients from society and, if possible, cure them, but also to protect society from the patients. For the sake of economy and efficiency, the present system of enormous hospitals has developed. Because of budgets, these hospitals must rely on partially trained personnel who work with patients that have limited contact with doctors. Goffman developed the concept of ***total institution*** to refer to "places of residence and work where a large number of like-situated individuals, cut off from the wider society for an appreciable period of time, together lead an enclosed, formally administered round of life." Mental hospitals qualify as such institutions

Due to the increased use of chemotherapy, ***community psychology*** developed during the 1960s. Community psychology entails easily accessible, locally controlled facilities that care for people in their own communities. The cornerstone of community psychology is the ***halfway house***, a small, privately run residential community, usually located in an urban area, in which ex-patients are helped to make the transition from the hospital to normal life.

Since those who suffer the most from mental disorders tend to gravitate toward public mental-health systems, the cost of caring for them is also shifting to those systems. The public system, however, cannot afford them. This contributes to a two-class mental-health system in which those most in need are undertreated.

Deinstitutionalization and homelessness are decidedly linked. Expanded welfare programs, increased use of psychotropic drugs, fiscal crises, and increased concern about patients rights contributed to fewer hospitalizations of mentally ill people. Combined with decreased availability of inexpensive housing, increasing numbers of mentally ill became homeless.

Social Policy

The political battles surrounding mental health care in the United States focus largely on the issue of parity, or eliminating the discrimination against mental illness that is inherent in existing health insurance plans.

Future prospects in the absence of a comprehensive approach to health care do not bode well, and it is likely that there will be further deterioration in the treatment conditions for people which severe mental illnesses. The mass murder at Virginia Technical University in Blacksburg, Virginia raises once again the question of how society can protect itself against psychotic killers and whether we are neglecting mental illness. One promising approach to the problem of the severely mentally ill is being promoted by the National Alliance for the Mentally Ill. They call for a program of assertive community treatment (PCT) for people with severe and persistent mental illnesses.

Going Beyond Left and Right

Whose responsibilities are the mentally ill? There may be no ideological debate over the need to end the warehousing of mentally ill people in isolated state hospitals, especially now with the new drug therapies. But where are they to live? Family responsibility and adequate funding of public programs need not be incompatible policies.

RESEARCH NAVIGATOR EXERCISES

ContentSelect
Use the sociology database, and enter the keyword *mental illness*. One recent and very interesting article deals with helping family members in dealing with schizophrenia (AN 25910429, 6/15/2007). After you have read the article, summarize the advice that is given to family members by the authors.

New York Times Online
Use sociology as the subject, and enter the keyword *mental illness*. Read the article entitled "Socially Anxious? Or Just Plain Shy? (9/27/2007). As an emotional and behavioral illness, how does social anxiety cause severe impairment in human functioning?

Link Library
Use sociology as the subject, and click on H for health care, and then click on National Institutes of Health-Health Information. This will take you to the National Institutes for Health homepage. Next, under the title National Institutes for Health, look for the navigation bar and click on institutes. On that page, look for the Quick Links, and click on NIMH. This will take you to the National Institute for Mental Health. On the home page for NIMH, look for the campaign on depression in men, Real Men, Real Depression. If this is not on the homepage, use the search command to find the topic of depression in men. Read about this topic. Do you recognize the symptoms of depression in yourself or others? Why do you think that depression in men often goes unrecognized and untreated? Why do you think that NIMH chose this particular title for their campaign? Are you surprised at the incidence of depression in men, and why do you think that their symptoms are often different than those of women?

PRACTICE TEST

MULTIPLE CHOICE QUESTIONS: Select the one best answer for each of the following questions.

1. In the United States, the most common forms of mental problems are:
   a. schizophrenia and paranoia.
   b. panic attacks and phobias.
   c. autism and epilepsy.
   d. alcoholism and substance abuse.

2. The interactionist perspective on mental illness focuses on:
   a. class variation in forms of mental illness.
   b. the latent functions of mental illness.
   c. the social construction of mental illness.
   d. the physiological causes of mental illness.

3. The rate of suicide, especially among teenagers and young adults:
   a. has increased steadily since the 1950s.
   b. has declined steadily since the 1950s.
   c. has remained the same since the 1950s.
   d. has been relatively low since the 1950s.

4. The view that mental disorder is a disease with biological causes is:
   a. the drift hypothesis.
   b. the residual deviance model.
   c. the medical model.
   d. the psychotropic theory.

5. The concept of mental disorder as deviance is that the disorder may be a function not only of a certain individual's inability to comply with societal expectations, but also:
   a. a function of the label attached to those who deviate.
   b. a justification for institutionalization.
   c. a function of social class.
   d. a problems in living issue.

6. The work of Thomas Szasz, who argues that mental illness is a myth, has called attention to the relationship between:
   a. class and institutionalization.
   b. diagnosis and repression.
   c. poverty and mental disorders.
   d. race and diagnosis.

7. Labeling theorists would tend to argue that application of medical diagnoses of mental illness:
   a. reflects cultural values, not scientific analysis.
   b. has improved our ability to treat specific forms of mental illness.
   c. demonstrates clear advances in treatment.
   d. is based on social class, race, or sex.

8. Conflict theorists call attention to differences in access to effective treatment for mental disorders based on:
   a. diagnostic classification.
   b. conflicts between law enforcement agencies and mental health agencies.
   c. inequalities in wealth and power.
   d. recent movement towards deinstitutionalization.

9. The Midtown Manhattan Study looked at 1,660 residents of midtown Manhattan and concluded that:
   a. children of upper-class parents tended to be more neurotic.
   b. children suffer from mental illness at the same rates as adults.
   c. socioeconomic status is a poor predictor of mental illness among children.
   d. socioeconomic status has a strong influence on the mental health of children.

10. The drift hypothesis suggests that the relationship between mental illness and social class is due to:
   a. mentally ill people not being capable of focusing on class issues.
   b. arbitrary definitions of social class.
   c. the inability to measure rates of mental illness.
   d. mentally ill people not able to function at the higher class level.

11. Research on the relationship between mental disorder and urban life has:
   a. proved conclusively that mental illness is caused by urban living.
   b. found that mental illness is more prevalent in urban settings.
   c. found equal incidence of mental illness in urban and rural settings.
   d. is one of the better understood relationships in the study of mental disorder.

12. Sociologists who study the relationship between race and mental illness have shown that:
   a. race appears to be a significant predictor of mental illness.
   b. race is NOT a significant variable by itself.
   c. blacks and Hispanics have higher rates of mental illness.
   d. whites are less likely to seek help for mental disorders.

13. Sociologists who study the relationship between race and mental illness have shown that:
   a. women are more likely than men to suffer from depression, anxieties, and phobias.
   b. men are more likely than women to suffer from depression, anxieties, and phobias.
   c. women are more likely than men to suffer from all forms of mental illness.
   d. men are more likely than women to suffer from all forms of mental illness.

14. Two major approaches to the treatment of mental disorders are:
   a. psychotherapy and psychotropic treatments.
   b. institutionalization and community psychology.
   c. individual and group therapy.
   d. psychotropic and chemotherapy.

15. A nonmedical form of treatment is:
   a. psychoanalysis.
   b. electroshock therapy.
   c. institutionalization.
   d. psychotropic therapy.

16. The most recent national-level study on mental illnesses found that the ______ of mental disorders in the United States did not change significantly from 1990 to 2003, but the ____ of treatment increased.
   a. rate, incidence
   b. mode, median usage
   c. prevalence, rate
   d. type, intensity

17. Long-term studies have shown that hospitalized patients who do not improve enough to be discharged within a short period are:
   a. treated effectively in halfway houses.
   b. likely to remain in the hospital for long periods of time.
   c. often misdiagnosed when initially admitted to the hospital.
   d. more likely to be women.

18. A total institution is characterized by:
    a. cutting off residents from the wider society.
    b. the voluntary total commitment made by its residents.
    c. the stringent entrance requirements.
    d. the community psychology used to treat residents.

19. Rosenhan (1973) found that pseudopatients admitted to mental hospitals:
    a. were recognized as such by staff and released.
    b. were recognized as normal by other patients, but not by staff.
    c. began to develop symptoms.
    d. developed unique ways of coping.

20. Halfway houses:
    a. provide housing for mentally ill homeless people.
    b. usually have close working relationships with mental hospitals.
    c. are designed to help people transition from the hospital to normal life.
    d. help ease the administrative burdens for mental hospitals.

ESSAY QUESTIONS

1. Compare and contrast how interactionists, functionalists, and conflict theorists view mental disorders.

2. Discuss the medical model and identify some of the benefits from viewing mental illness from this perspective.

3. Discuss labeling theory as applied to mental illness and identify criticisms labeling theorists have made of the medical model.

4. Identify some of the factors that have led to increased deinstitutionalization of the mentally ill.

5. What were the findings and conclusions of the Midtown Manhattan Study?

6. Differentiate between and provide illustrations for the terms incidences and rates.

7. What does Goffman's research on total institutions suggest about the treatment of patients in mental hospitals?

8. Why do you think eating disorders such as anorexia nervosa and bulimia, and cognitive disorders such as ADHD and ADD, are becoming more common in our society?

ANSWERS TO MULTIPLE CHOICE QUESTIONS

1.	b	11.	b
2.	c	12.	b
3.	a	13.	a
4.	c	14.	a
5.	a	15.	a
6.	b	16.	c
7.	a	17.	b
8.	c	18.	a
9.	d	19.	b
10.	d	20.	c

CHAPTER FOUR

Alcohol and Other Drugs

CHAPTER OUTLINE

I. The Nature of the Problem
  A. Drug Abuse
  B. Abuse, Addiction, and Dependence
II. Alcohol Use and Abuse
  A. Problem Drinkers and Alcoholics
  B. Who Drinks?
    1. Biological Factors
    2. Socioeconomic Factors
    3. Gender
    4. Age
    5. Religion
    6. Cultural Influences
  C. Drinking among Young People
    1. Binge Drinking
  D. Alcohol-Related Social Problems
    1. Health
    2. Drinking and Driving
    3. Alcohol and Arrest Rates
    4. Effects on the Family
    5. Alcoholism and Homelessness
  E. Treatment of Alcoholism
    1. Rehabilitation
    2. Alcoholics Anonymous
    3. Antabuse
    4. Other Programs
    5. The Johnson Intervention
III. Illegal Drug Use and Abuse
  A. Commonly Abused Drugs
    1. Marijuana
    2. Cocaine
    3. Heroin
    4. Hallucinogens
    5. Amphetamines
    6. Ecstasy, Methamphetamine, and Other "Designer Drugs"
    7. Abuse of Prescription Drugs
  B. Patterns of Drug Abuse
    1. Who Uses Drugs?
    2. How Does Drug Use Spread?
  C. Drug Abuse, Crime, and Violence
  D. Drug Use and AIDS
  E. Treatment of Drug Abuse
    1. Therapeutic Communities
    2. Methadone Maintenance

3. Narcotic Antagonists

IV. Social Policy

A. Future Prospects

V. Going Beyond Left and Right

VI. Summary

VII. Key Terms

VIII. Social Problems Online

IX. Research Navigator

LEARNING OBJECTIVES

After reading Chapter Four you should:

1. Be aware of the difference between a pharmacological and a sociological definition for the term "drug."
2. Be able to define drug abuse, addiction, dependence, and prevalence.
3. Know the facts about alcohol abuse and use in this country.
4. Be familiar with research on problem drinkers and how researchers define problem drinking and alcoholism.
5. Know the data on who is most likely to drink, and how demographic and socioeconomic variables affect this likelihood.
6. Know the facts about drinking and young people.
7. Know what social problems are related to alcohol.
8. Be familiar with the treatment options for alcoholism.
9. Be able to identify and discuss commonly used illegal drugs.
10. Be familiar with the patterns of drug abuse, including who uses drugs and how drug use spreads.
11. Know how drug use is linked to crime and violence.
12. Know the facts about AIDS and drug use.
13. Be familiar with the three major techniques for treating drug abuse.
14. Be familiar with the social policy issues regarding drug and alcohol use and abuse in the United States.

KEY TERMS

drug
drug abuse
addiction
psychological dependence
habituation
prevalence
alcoholics
codependency
detoxified
aversion therapy
behavior conditioning
narcotic antagonists

CHAPTER SUMMARY

The Nature of the Problem

Ours is a drug-using society. We use drugs to escape pain, increase alertness, relax tension, lose weight, gain strength, fight depression, and avoid pregnancy. Abuse of alcohol and other drugs is a growing problem throughout the world. One in four deaths of men aged 15 to 29 in Europe is due to alcohol, and opiate and cocaine addiction is a growing problem. The sociological definition of the term ***drug*** denotes any habit-forming substance that directly affects the brain or nervous system; this broad definition includes some substances that are not classified as a drug in society, such as alcohol and tobacco, but which have been proven harmful.

Drug abuse is the use of unacceptable drugs and/or the excessive or inappropriate use of acceptable drugs in ways that can lead to physical, psychological, or social harm. There is both an objective and a subjective component to drug use, which are not always in agreement. The objective component refers to the extent to which a given substance causes physiological, psychological, or social problems for the individual or for the society. The subjective component refers to how people perceive the drug and how these perceptions result in social action concerning drug use.

Objectively, we know that simple drugs like aspirin are overused and abused. Subjectively, however, this is not seen as a problem of abuse. In other cases, a drug (e.g., marijuana) may not be especially harmful objectively, but may be perceived to be a danger. The discrepancy between the objective and the subjective comes to prominence quite often in American politics. The discrepancy is also evident in the contradiction between research on the damaging effects of nicotine and alcohol and the fact that these drugs continue to be legal.

The term ***addiction*** is used to describe a complex phenomenon involving physical dependence on a drug, which means the user will suffer upon discontinuation of the drug, whereas ***psychological dependence***, or ***habituation,*** occurs when the user needs a drug for the feeling of well-being that it produces. Addiction can be dangerous to society when it becomes widespread enough to reduce labor markets and create underground drug economies. Social scientific data are important in monitoring the prevalence of drug use.

The DSM-IV carefully defines the terms dependence and abuse, as these definitions are used to determine third-party payments for treatment and to legally determine the presence of alcohol problems. Not all drug use is problematic when it impairs health: for example, the terminally ill may be addicted to morphine for pain relief but would not be considered an abuser.

Knowledge of patterns of use is crucial; so much research focuses on ***prevalence***, or the estimated population of people suffering from a given condition at any given time. **Table 4-1** shows data on the lifetime prevalence rates of use of different drugs among high school seniors in 2006. **Figure 4-1** illustrates the illicit drug use by age for the years 1979-2003.

In American society, people have mixed feelings about alcohol. On the one hand, it is viewed positively and has economic benefits. On the other hand, the problems created by abuse are staggering. In recent years, the American people have become more aware of problems associated with drinking; this awareness has led to crusades against excessive drinking.

Research suggests that 8.46 percent of the adults in the United States meet the criteria for alcoholism and an alcoholic family member has affected 76 million. ***Alcoholics*** have an uncontrollable need for intoxication, and if this need is frustrated will develop acute withdrawal symptoms.

Genetic factors linked to alcoholism are able to explain about half the risk for alcoholism. Social factors that affect alcoholism and problem drinking include age, gender, religion, and socioeconomic status. In general, heavy drinkers tend to be younger. Those who attend church appear to drink less. Women tend to have lower rates of drinking problems, although the rate has been increasing among adult women in recent years. Binge drinking tends to be a problem among males. Binge drinking among pregnant women is a problem because of the danger to fetal health. Those with higher SES drink less than those with lower SES. Businessmen drink more than farmers; among women, service workers drink most heavily. Additionally, there are cultural and biological factors that impact the use and abuse of alcohol. Drinking among college and high school students is considered to be a social problem. The influence of groups, especially families, is a powerful determinant of drinking behavior. Advertising, even those promoting moderation, also have an impact on drinking by reinforcing the idea that consumption is a reward for hard work, a form of escape, a means of promoting romance, and a way of obtaining comradeship.

Drinking by teenagers and young adults is a serious social problem. Teenage problem drinkers are defined by problems with teachers and police because of their drinking. Only a small proportion of these can be defined as chronically alcoholic. Binge drinking among high school and college students is also a problem. Many college students engage in binge drinking, and they have higher rates of alcohol-related deaths and injuries. Research on this group defines binge drinking as more than five drinks for men and more than four drinks for women in a sitting.

A 1999 study found that 44 percent reported at least one episode of heavy drinking in the year prior to the survey. Because of alcohol-related deaths and injuries, many states have passed laws raising the minimum age for drinking.

There are many factors contributing to the popularity of drinking among young people: the difficulty of obtaining other drugs, low legal drinking ages, alcohol products designed for young people, and peer pressure. In addition, young people may drink for the same reasons as older adults.

Excessive use of alcohol contributes to a number of social problems and costs about $130 billion annually. Alcohol abuse has an impact on the health of abusers and their families; it impacts crime, homelessness, and the rate of traffic accidents. Alcoholics can expect to live 10 to 12 fewer years than nonalcoholics. Alcohol has been implicated in about 40 percent of all traffic fatalities, and about 12 percent of all nonserious crime arrests.

Within the family, children may develop severe physical and emotional problems and may experience ***codependency***. Codependency means that the spouse of the problem drinker, and often the children as well, frequently participate in a pattern of interaction designed to excuse the problematic behavior. Alcoholism is present in about 5 percent of the homeless population.

There are a number of approaches to treatment that have had various levels of success. These include rehabilitation, Alcoholics Anonymous, Antabuse, the Johnson Intervention, and other programs. Alcoholism is increasingly viewed as an illness, which suggests that it is possible to rehabilitate alcoholics. Federal programs and hospitals are developing ways to treat alcoholics with rehabilitation in mind.

Alcoholics Anonymous has about 2 million members who attempt to manage their alcoholism through acknowledging their lack of control over alcohol and abstain completely. Alcoholics Anonymous has spawned associated groups that help family members deal with the alcoholism of other family members. The success of Alcoholics Anonymous may, in part, be due to the fact that memberships are voluntary, which suggests they may be more highly motivated.

Antabuse is a drug that causes uncomfortable physical symptoms when taken with alcohol. It has been used to treat alcoholics, but critics argue that it does not address the underlying personality problems of the drinker. Alcoholics are ***detoxified*** when they are kept off alcohol until none shows in blood samples. ***Aversion therapy*** or ***behavior conditioning*** involves treatment programs that condition the patient against alcohol through nausea-producing drugs or shock therapy.

Community-based programs that help drinkers remain in their job while under treatment have better results than institutionalization. Employee assistance programs have demonstrated considerable effectiveness in treating problem drinkers in the workplace. The Johnson Intervention is a tough love approach that has been successful in getting problem drinkers to enter and complete treatment.

Illegal Drug Use and Abuse

Trends in drug use change quite rapidly, but the most serious social problems associated with illegal drug use have always stemmed from drugs that cause severe psychological and physiological addictions. There are numerous illegal drugs that have some prevalence in American society; these include marijuana, cocaine, heroin, amphetamines, ecstasy and other designer drugs, and barbiturates.

Marijuana is a social drug with widespread use and with little evidence of detrimental long-term effects. The federal government has shifted law-enforcement attention to more addictive drugs.

Cocaine, which produces a sense of greater strength and endurance and a feeling of increased intellectual power, can cause paranoid psychoses when taken in large quantities over time. Because it originally had a higher street price, it tended to be used more by upper classes. However, in recent years its use has become more prevalent in middle and working classes. Crack, a form of cocaine that can be smoked, has peaked in use, but it is still very popular. Violence and birth defects associated with crack are still serious problems in some communities.

Heroin causes users to feel sudden, intense feelings of pleasure; others may feel greater self-esteem and composure. The typical heroin addict is under age 30, lives in urban settings, and must resort to property crime to support his or her habit. Withdrawal symptoms are very unpleasant, and addicts avoid withdrawal at all costs. Evidence suggests that heroin use is again on the rise.

Hallucinogens, such as LSD (lysergic acid diethylamide), are drugs that distort the user's perceptions. No data indicate that LSD can cause either physical or emotional dependence. Studies indicate that long-term adverse reactions to LSD occur primarily when the user has pre-existing mental problems.

Amphetamines are legal when prescribed by a physician, and many people become addicted to them through medical use. Amphetamine-like drugs, e.g., Ritalin, are increasingly prescribed for hyperactive children.

Ecstasy, methamphetamine, and other "designer drugs" are drugs related to amphetamines and are produced in illegal chemical laboratories. Research shows that Ecstasy can produce serious illness and even death. Recent data show that teenagers are beginning to increase their wariness and disapproval of these drugs; however, they are still popular party drugs.

Abuse of prescription drugs is becoming an ever more serious form of drug use and addiction. For examples, barbiturates depress the central nervous system and can create physical addiction with symptoms similar to heroin addiction. These are often taken with, or alternated with, amphetamines, thereby making the normal rhythm of life meaningless.

The opportunity to use drugs is among the most important factors in illicit use. Age is also an important factor as teenagers and young adults are most likely to use them. Two important sources of information on drug use are the Monitoring the Future survey and the National Household Survey on Drug Abuse. These surveys have also shown that men more than women, whites more than other groups, lower classes more than upper classes, and younger more than older people use drugs.

Data from national surveys indicate that drug use peaked in the 1970s, declined, and then increased again in the 1990s, although it hasn't reached the levels of the 1970s. Alcohol use among teenagers and young adults is the most prevalent. Surveys of drug use over time provide information about its distribution by gender, economic status, and racial or ethnic background, although some of the results are mixed and it is important to look at proportions as well as absolute numbers of users. Research by Lloyd Johnson finds that there is a negative relationship between disapproval and tendency to use drugs among teenagers. **Figure 4-6** and **Table 4-2** show data concerning attitudes toward and patterns of drug use among different categories of people looking at such variables as age, gender, socioeconomic status, and racial and ethnic background.

Most sociologists and social psychologists agree that drug use is a learned behavior that spreads through groups of peers who influence one another. Most research shows that marijuana is not a steppingstone to other drugs. Other factors may set the stage for involvement in drug-using peer groups. These include the individual's socioeconomic status and neighborhood environment, and the influences of family, religion, and school.

A disease model concerning the spread of heroin was developed identifying "initiators" and "susceptible communities," and suggested ways to identify and contain the "contagious" individuals. Some studies suggest that people are able to abstain from extremely addictive drugs when their social milieu supports nonuse.

Drug use is related to crime and violence, but this relationship varies by type of drug. Heroin and crack cocaine are most frequently associated with criminal behavior. Over 80 percent of all prison inmates have a history of substance abuse, and about 50 percent of those arrested from crimes are drug users. Drug use is also related to AIDS, but efforts to prevent this have often met opposition.

Needle exchange programs do seem to work; outreach programs face resistance from the public and from the users themselves. A number of treatment methods have been tried, including therapeutic community-based treatments, methadone for heroin addicts, and the use of narcotic antagonists to negate the effects produced by opiates. Social policies that address drug and alcohol abuse take two forms: control strategies and law enforcement.

Drug use spreads through the peer group and may be reversed with a change in social milieu. For example, even crack addicts have been helped by a change from the social milieu in which the drug is used.

Therapeutic communities offer a social milieu that enables individuals to re-enter social life gradually at their own pace. The Phoenix House is based on a therapeutic community that relies on ex-addicts to help addicts break through the barriers of isolation and hostility.

Methadone is a synthetic narcotic that can help heroin addicts with the withdrawal symptoms of heroin. It is now used regularly in treatment programs.

Narcotic antagonists are substances that negate the effects produced by opiates. By counteracting the positive sensations produced by heroin, narcotic antagonists help motivated addicts overcome their psychological conditioning to the drug.

Social Policy

Social policies that address drug and alcohol abuse take on two main forms: control strategies and law enforcement strategies. This section focuses on law enforcement strategies. Approaches to law enforcement include cracking down on sale or use of drugs, and legalization of some drugs and other revisions to drug laws. Some of these efforts have met with success, others have caused controversy between local and federal authorities or have raised concerns about civil liberties. Other law enforcement efforts are focused on foreign policy and potential sanctions against drug-exporting countries. There are almost no prospects for a full-scale evaluation and review of the failure of the so-called "War on Drugs."

Going Beyond Left and Right

Is there really a difference between the views of those on the left and right? There are differences, but there are no monolithic views on either side of the political spectrum. On the other hand, there are clear differences among segments of our population. Four statements expressing beliefs concerning certain issues relating to drugs and alcohol are identified that seem to clearly differentiate among these segments.

RESEARCH NAVIGATOR EXERCISES

ContentSelect

Select the sociology database and use the keyword *alcoholism*. In conjunction with the text's discussion of *binge drinking*, read Coleman et. al.'s article (*AN 2572739*) (August, 2007) on the subject. What suggestions do the authors have for changing the culture of young people's binge drinking and what are your reactions to their proposals? Do you think the suggestions are promising……not promising?

New York Times Online

Use sociology as the subject, and enter the keywords *drunk driving*. Look for the 9/23/07 article,

"Drunken Driving Fatalities Steadily Rise." Read about the increase in deaths due to drunk driving and problems faced by states and the government in trying to achieve further reductions. What new or novel strategies can you think of that might reduce drunk driving?

Link Library
Use sociology as the subject. Click on A for alcohol abuse. Click on alcoholism (clearinghouse of information on alcohol abuse from About.com). Scroll down in the subjects column to women and alcohol. Read about a variety of issues dealing with women and alcohol especially female drinking and brain damage and health risks for women. Do you think our society focuses more on men's drinking problems than women's? Do you believe that women are being neglected in the research literature? Why or why not?

PRACTICE TEST

MULTIPLE CHOICE QUESTIONS: Select the one best answer for each of the following questions.

1. Drug abuse refers to:
   a. use of unacceptable or illicit drugs.
   b. excessive or inappropriate use of illicit drugs.
   c. use of unacceptable and/or excessive or inappropriate use of acceptable drugs in ways that can lead to physical, psychological, or social harm.
   d. excessive use of drugs other than alcohol.

2. Addiction commonly refers to
   a. psychological dependence.
   b. habituation.
   c. codependency.
   d. physical dependence.

3. The estimated population of people suffering from a given condition at any given time is referred to as:
   a. prevalence.
   b. dependence.
   c. abuse.
   d. habituation.

4. According to the National Institute on Drug Abuse (NIDA) lifetime prevalence rates of use of different drugs among high school seniors finds _____ to be the most commonly used drug.
   a. cigarettes
   b. alcohol
   c. marijuana
   d. inhalants

5. Alcohol is implicated in about __ percent of all fatal highway accidents in the United States.
   a. 20
   b. 40
   c. 60
   d. 80

6. Recent decades have seen alcoholism among adult women:
   a. decrease somewhat.
   b. decrease dramatically.
   c. increase somewhat.
   d. increase dramatically.

7. When children grow up with routine, comfortable exposure to alcohol within the family, they are:
   a. more likely to become excessive drinkers.
   b. less likely to become excessive drinkers.
   c. more likely to seek treatment for alcoholism.
   d. less likely to allow their own children to drink alcohol.

8. The Harvard School of Public Health College Alcohol Survey (CAS) defines binge drinking as the consumption of ___ or more drinks in a single session for males and as ___ drinks in one session for females.
   a. 5;4 c. 7;5
   b. 3;2 d. 8;7

9. On average, alcoholics can expect to live ______ years fewer than nonalcoholics.
   a. 6 to 8
   b. 10 to 12
   c. 14 to 16
   d. 20 to 22

10. About ____ percent of arrests for all nonserious crimes involve drunkenness.
   a. 2 c. 32
   b. 12 d. 42

11. Most alcoholics and problem drinkers:
   a. are homeless vagrants.
   b. have jobs and families.
   c. were homeless before they developed the drinking problem.
   d. transition to homelessness over a period of years.

12. One factor that may contribute to the success of Alcoholics Anonymous is:
   a. voluntary participation.
   b. aversion therapy.
   c. Antabuse.
   d. Alateen, and similar programs for dependents of alcoholics.

13. _____ is a prescription drug that sensitizes the patient in such a way that consuming even a small quantity of alcohol causes strong and uncomfortable physical symptoms.
   a. Antabuse c. Detoxim
   b. Elevil d. Aversium

14. Trends in the major categories of illegal drugs:
   a. have remained constant over the last century.
   b. are constantly changing as culture and customs change.
   c. have merged toward the use of cocaine.
   d. are correlated with the use of marijuana.

15. The acknowledged relationship between heroin and crime results:
   a. directly from the influence of the drug.
   b. from addicts wanting to avoid the withdrawal symptoms.
   c. indirectly from a heroin culture among criminals.
   d. from heroin use among the prison population.

16. Which of the following drugs is classified as a hallucinogen?
    a. marijuana
    b. amphetamines
    c. barbiturates
    d. LSD

17. Over ___ percent of all prison inmates have a history of substance abuse.
    a. 20
    b. 40
    c. 60
    d. 80

18. Which of the following statements concerning drug treatment is correct?
    a. Once an addict, always an addict.
    b. There are no successful treatment programs.
    c. Changing an addict's social environment is essential.
    d. none of the above

19. As a therapeutic community, the _______ approach rests on two key precepts: that addicts must assume responsibility for their own actions and that treatment should address psychological as well as physical difficulties.
    a. Phoenix House
    b. Cleveland House
    c. Tampa House
    d. North Bay House

20. Which of the following strategies has been used to decrease alcohol-related motor vehicle fatalities?
    a. increase the age of legal drinking
    b. educational programs for first time offenders
    c. sobriety checks on the roads
    d. all of the above

ESSAY QUESTIONS

1. Distinguish among drug abuse, dependence, and addiction.

2. Discuss alcohol use and abuse; make sure to describe those factors that influence who drinks, how much, and in what ways.

3. Discuss treatments for alcoholism.

4. List and discuss the most commonly used illegal drugs.

5. Discuss the link between drug use and crime and drug use and AIDS.

6. Define the term drug and then go on to explain what is meant by drug abuse, addiction, and dependence. Be sure to provide examples.

7. Identify and describe some the most commonly used and abused illegal drugs.

8. Identify and describe some of the methods used to treat alcoholism.

9. What is the relationship between drugs and crime?

10. Describe patterns of illegal drug use. Who uses illegal drugs?

ANSWERS TO MULTIPLE CHOICE QUESTIONS

1.	c	11.	b
2.	d	12.	a
3.	a	13.	d
4.	b	14.	b
5.	b	15.	b
6.	d	16.	d
7.	a	17.	d
8.	c	18.	c
9.	b	19.	d
10.	d	20.	a

CHAPTER FIVE

Crime and Violence

CHAPTER OUTLINE

I. The Nature of Crime
   A. Police Discretion
   B. Problems of Accuracy
II. Types of Crimes and Criminals
   A. Violent Personal Crimes
      1. Criminal Homicide
      2. Mass Murderers and Serial Killers
   B. Occasional Property Crimes
   C. Occupational (White-Collar) Crimes
      1. Embezzlement
      2. Fraud
   D. Corporate Crimes
   E. Public-Order Crimes
   F. Organized Crimes
      1. Organized Crime and Corruption
   G. Conventional and Professional Crimes
      1. Cybercrime
      2. Identity Theft
   H. Juvenile Delinquency
   I. Hate Crimes
III. Gangs, Guns, and Violent Death
   A. Gangs and Violence
   B. Recent Trends
IV. Conditions and Causes of Crime and Violence
   A. Biological Explanations of Crime
   B. Biology, Violence, and Criminality
   C. Gender and Crime
   D. Age and Crime
      1. Violent Youth Crime
   E. Sociological Explanations of Crime
      1. Conflict Approaches to the Study of Crime
      2. The Functionalist View: Anomie Theory
      3. Interactionist Approaches: Differential Association and Delinquent Subcultures
V. Controlling Crime
   A. Retribution-Deterrence
   B. Rehabilitation
   C. Prevention
VI. Social Policy
   A. Mandatory Sentencing
   B. Arrest and Incarceration
      1. The Prison Paradox
      2. Racial Disparities in Sentencity
      3. Alternatives to Incarceration

C. Occupational and Corporate Crimes
D. Organized Crime
E. Public-Order and Juvenile-Justice Reforms
F. Gun Control
G. Future Prospects

VII. Going Beyond Left and Right
VIII. Summary
IX. Key Terms
X. Social Problems Online
XI. Research Navigator

LEARNING OBJECTIVES

After reading Chapter Five you should:

1. Understand the difficulty of defining crime, but be familiar with crime as defined in the text.
2. Understand the distinction between criminal and civil law.
3. Be familiar with the Uniform Crime Reports and the crime index.
4. Be aware of the importance of police discretion and the impact it has on who is arrested.
5. Be aware of problems of accuracy in crime statistics; know why statistics may not be accurate.
6. Know how crime is categorized; be able to distinguish the following types of crime: violent personal, occasional property, occupational, corporate, public order, conventional, organized, professional, juvenile delinquency, hate.
7. Be aware of the relationship between gang membership and guns and violent death.
8. Be familiar with the biological approach to explaining crime and its shortcomings.
9. Know how gender, age, race, and crime are linked.
10. Be familiar with sociological explanations for crime, including the conflict approach, the functionalist approach (anomie theory), and interactionist approaches (differential association and deviant subcultures).
11. Be able to identify and describe the four strategies for controlling crime: retribution, deterrence, rehabilitation, and prevention.
12. Be knowledgeable about the social policy implications associated with conventional, occupational and corporate, organized and public-order crimes, and juvenile delinquency and gun control.

KEY TERMS

crime index
crime
criminal law
civil law
victimization reports
murder
manslaughter
differential association
embezzlement
fraud
organized crime
status offenses

anomie
social control
recidivism
plea bargaining
probation
parole

CHAPTER SUMMARY

Americans regard crime as a serious social problem and spend heavily to control crime. The prison population in the United States has reached record proportions. Emile Durkheim observed that crime is actually normal, as it exists wherever there are people and laws. According to the Uniform Crime Reports published by the FBI, between 2005 and 2006 there was a 1.3 percent increase in serious crime. Although it is too soon to know exactly, this finding may mark the end of the rather steady downward trend in crime that occurred during the economic boom years of the 1990s

Crime is hard to measure as is indicated by inconsistencies in two major sources of data, the Uniform Crime Report and the National Crime Victimization Survey; the NCVS shows higher rates, as illustrated in **Figure 5-2**.

The extent of the nation's crime problem is measured by the ***crime index***. The crime index collects data on the most serious and most frequently occurring crimes—those that are most likely to come to the attention of the police. These include murder and nonnegligent manslaughter, forcible rape, robbery, aggravated assault, burglary, larceny-theft, motor vehicle theft, and arson. **Figure 5-5** reveals the "crime clock," which represents the annual ratio of crime to fixed time intervals.

The Nature of Crime

There is no single, universally agreed-upon definition of crime. One definition for ***crime*** is an act or omission of an act for which the state can apply sanctions. ***Criminal law*** prohibits certain acts and prescribes the punishment to be meted out to violators. ***Civil law*** deals with noncriminal acts in which one person injures another; these are mediated by the state. Many white-collar (or occupational) crimes and organized crimes remain difficult to assess.

The police exert considerable discretion in the application of law. Some studies, e.g., Chambliss' research on the Saints and the Roughnecks, reveal police bias in arrests. One controversy over official statistics concerns the rates of criminality by social class; some data suggest that rates may not be different for lower- and upper-class offenders.

Official data on crime depend on crime reports from police reports, which vary in level and quality. Consequently, official data may not give an accurate picture of the actual rates of crime. Researchers have tried to overcome this problem. These techniques suggest that the distribution of criminal behavior may be different than reported by Uniform Crime Report statistics, e.g., race is less of a factor.

Victimization reports have also been developed (e.g., National Crime Victimization Survey). These surveys ask respondents about being victims of crime. These studies suggest that some crimes, e.g., sex crimes, are underreported in official statistics. Also, crime may be underreported in low-income, high-crime areas where victims are less likely to file reports.

Types of Crimes and Criminals

There are nine major types of crime and criminals. These are violent personal crime (e.g., assault, robbery, homicide); occasional property crimes (e.g., vandalism, check forging, shoplifting); occupational or white-collar crimes (e.g., embezzlement and fraud); corporate crime (e.g., insider trading, environmental crimes); public-order crimes (e.g., prostitution, gambling, traffic violations); conventional crimes and professional crimes (e.g., robbery, larceny, burglary, counterfeiting, blackmail); organized crime (e.g., loan-sharking, drug trafficking); juvenile delinquency (gangs, drug activity, running away);

and hate crimes (e.g., intimidation, vandalism, destruction of property, aggravated assault).

Violent personal crimes include assault, robbery, and various types of homicide acts in which physical injury is inflicted or threatened. The level of deadly violence is higher in the United States than in any other urban industrial nation. Drugs and guns are important contributing factors, but others point to the pervasiveness of violence in our culture.

There are two types of criminal homicide: murder and manslaughter. ***Murder*** is distinguished by unlawful killing with malice aforethought. ***Manslaughter*** is unlawful homicide without malice or aforethought.

Most murderers are not career criminals, but there are social patterns to murder. Murders are most likely to occur in large cities; most murderers are young men. More than half of all murder victims are minorities; someone of the same race murders most. A family member or intimate acquaintance murders most murder victims. Finally, the murder rate for the mentally ill is not significant. The homicide rate in the United States is much higher than in other industrialized nations. One reason for this may be the availability of powerful firearms; gang activity is also a factor.

Mass murder is defined as the murder of four or more people at the same time; serial murder is when a series of murders are committed. Mass murderers tend to kill in a spontaneous fit of rage, whereas serial murderers seek to perfect their killing technique to prevent detection and apprehension. Most mass murderers are paranoid or sexual sadists.

Occasional property crimes include vandalism, check forgery, shoplifting, and some kinds of automobile theft. People who view themselves as law-abiding citizens usually commit these crimes. They tend not be habitual lawbreakers.

Occupational, or white-collar, crime is crime committed by people who break the law as part of their normal business activity. This crime rarely comes to the criminal courts and is rarely judged as severely as other kinds of crime. Further, the occupational criminal is far removed from the popular stereotype of a criminal. Sutherland's theory of ***differential association*** asserts that occupational criminality, like other forms of systematic criminal behavior, is learned through frequent direct or indirect association with people who are already engaging in such behavior.

Embezzlement is the theft from one's employer and usually committed by otherwise law-abiding people during the course of their employment. Three conditions seem to facilitate embezzlement: 1) financial problems that the individual doesn't want others to know about, 2) the opportunity, and 3) a formula for rationalizing the crime.

Fraud is obtaining money or property under false pretenses and can occur at any level of business and in any type of business relationship. Fraud committed through computer technology has increased dramatically and ranges from data diddling to super zapping.

Corporate crimes include, but are not limited to, environmental crimes, illegal credit card manipulations, insider trading in financial institutions, intimidation of competitors and employees, illegal labor practices, defrauding of pension plans, falsification of company records, bribery of public officials, and computer crime.

The largest case of corporate crime occurred in the 1980s with the savings and loan scandal. However, in 2002 authorities charged executives of Enron, Tyco, Arthur Andersen, WorldCom, and other firms with fraud and other criminal activities.

Public-order offenses include prostitution, gambling, use of illegal substances, drunkenness, vagrancy, disorderly conduct, and traffic violations. In terms of sheer numbers, this is the largest category of crime. Public-order offenders rarely consider themselves criminals or view their actions as crimes.

Prostitution is an example of a public-order crime, and some have argued for its legalization. They argue prostitution is a victimless crime, the laws are difficult to enforce and are enforced unequally, income would be taxable, and health codes could be applied. Others argue that prostitution is a crime against society and legalization would not have the benefits those who favor legalization suggest.

Organized crime is a system in which illegal activities are carried out as part of a rational plan devised by a large, often global organization that is attempting to maximize its overall profit.

Large, globally organized crime organizations derive huge profits from supplying illegal goods and services to the public. Their major source of profit is illegal gambling in the form of lotteries, numbers games, off-track betting, illegal casinos, and dice games. Organized crime could not flourish without bribery, which occurs at all levels of government.

Conventional offenders tend to be young adults who commit robbery, larceny, burglary, and gang theft as a way of life. They are semiprofessionals who frequently get away with crime and consequently begin to identify themselves with criminality. They are reinforced not only by the profit, but also by the lifestyle and excitement of crime. Because offenders associate mostly with other criminals, they develop a shared outlook that scorns the benefits of law-abiding behavior.

Professional criminals are dedicated to a life of crime; they live by it, and take pride in their accomplishments. They are rarely caught and, therefore, spend very little time in jail. They tend to come from higher social strata than other criminals.

Historically, children have been presumed to lack criminal intent, and a separate justice system has been developed for them. In recent years there have been criticisms of the juvenile justice system, but juvenile crime has actually been decreasing. This is due to the general aging of the population and the decline of the crack epidemic. Many young people become involved in the retail drug trade, which puts them at risk for becoming involved in other types of crime.

Teenagers who are arrested on minor sales or possession charges often begin a career in and out of detention centers and jails, where they are initiated into the world of the professional criminal.

Status offenses, such as running away and vagrancy, are very common reasons for arrests of juveniles. More females than males are arrested for running away; this is due to the fact that females are more likely to be abused at home.

Some crimes are motivated by deep hatred. Hatred of gays or people of other races is widespread in all societies, but the propensity to express it through violent acts tends to be a phenomenon of youth and young adulthood. The emotions that motivate such crimes are taken from the adults who socialize the young. **Table 5-1** shows the most common hate crimes.

Gangs, Guns, and Violent Death

Homicide rates in the United States have reached levels as much as twenty times that of other industrialized nations. The reason is partly explained by changing patterns of juvenile violence, the increase firepower available to violent people, and the inability of American society to agree on appropriate controls on lethal weapons. Not only is there gang violence in large cities that make headlines in the news media, but there has also been an upsurge of gang activity and gang-related violence in smaller cities and suburban areas.

Between 1960 and 1990 the rate of offenses involving dangerous weapons doubled. There is regional variation in this statistic, but the increase is also associated with the rise of gang violence. There is a wide range of gangs; some are street corner cliques, but others have evolved into well-organized, hierarchical crime syndicates. In small cities and suburbs gangs are a relatively new phenomenon or have not yet formed. Relationships between teenagers and police, the drug trade and its control, and how young people see the need to protect their turf are important determinants of how gangs will evolve.

Studies indicate that gangs would prefer to avoid violence, but members have a worldview that they must be aggressive or they will be attacked first. Moreover, they don't see any other way to achieve their goals. An increased availability of guns makes their use more likely. The question looms as to whether the United States is in the midst of a rise in violent youth gang activity.

Conditions and Causes of Crime and Violence

There are multiple theories and correlates of crime. In general, the evidence does not seem to strongly support biological arguments. Sociological theories of crime include conflict theory, anomie theory, differential association theory, and delinquent subculture. Other factors that influence crime are gender, race, and age.

Early research in the nineteenth century and before tried to identify physical characteristics of criminals on the assumption that they were physically different somehow. These theories have largely been discounted, although there is still research today that is attempting to identify genetic differences that identify criminals.

Homo sapiens are the earth's most dangerous living species. This has led to the question of whether violence is simply part of human nature. There is considerable evidence for social and psychological explanations of violence, but scientists continue to search for neurological explanations.

Men are more likely than women to commit crimes. However, this general gap has declined as women have gained greater social equality with men in industrialized countries. The differences in arrest rates seem to be the result of different patterns of socialization. Men are socialized to be more aggressive; the courts have tended to be more protective of women and are, therefore, less likely to arrest or convict women.

Criminologists have found age to be more strongly correlated with criminal behavior than any other factor, not only in terms of rates, but also in terms of the types of crime committed. Young people are arrested more than older offenders, some of which can be explained by teenagers and young people being enticed by the opportunities to commit various kinds of theft.

The rate of violent felonies committed by children aged 10 to 17 has increased for most of the past ten years, a trend that runs counter to the decrease in violence among adults in the United States. This has declined somewhat in the past few years, due, in part, to aging of the population in general and criminals maturing out of criminal lifestyles.

Three other approaches to explaining crime are based on 1) conflict theory, 2) functionalist perspectives, and 3) interactionist perspectives. There are incidences of crime among lower socioeconomic classes. For most of the twentieth century, it was believed that people in lower socioeconomic classes were more likely to commit crimes. However, analyses of self-reported data have found no evidence of this.

Some cross-culture studies suggest that rapid increases in inequality are associated with increased crime rates. Others argue that unequal treatment of drug and alcohol abuse is leading to increases in convictions.

Every study of crime based on official data shows that blacks are overrepresented among those who are arrested, convicted, and imprisoned for street crime. It could be that overrepresentation is due to greater surveillance of blacks, but victimization studies suggest that there is more crime in black communities. Conflict theorists focus on the loss of manufacturing jobs and unequal access to legal employment as an explanation.

Functionalists tend to look at the lack of access to socially approved means to achieve socially approved goals. ***Anomie***, the feeling of being adrift that arises from disparity between goals and means, may vary with nationality, ethnic background, bias, religion, and other social characteristics.

Interactionist explanations of criminal behavior focus on the processes by which individuals internalize norms that encourage criminality. According to proponents of differential association theory, criminal behavior is a result of a learning process that occurs chiefly within small, intimate groups. Some sociologists argue that the formation of delinquent subcultures is a frustrated reaction to exclusion by the larger society. Others reject this view and argue that delinquency is a product of lower-class culture which has specific views about trouble, toughness, smartness, excitement, fate, and autonomy.

Controlling Crime

Social control refers to the capacity of a social group to regulate itself according to principles beyond individual self-interest. Techniques can range from the very informal, such as gossip, to the very formal, such as the criminal justice system. Formal efforts to control crime can be categorized under four headings: retribution-deterrence, rehabilitation, prevention, and reform of the criminal justice system.

Retribution and deterrence have historically been the primary focus of controlling crime. Punishment is meant to serve several purposes. It is meant to deter crime, but it also sustains morale of those who conform to society's rules by creating the sense that those who do not make the sacrifices associated with conforming do not get away with it. Some criminologists emphasize the importance of the moral stigmatism associated with crime. Without the stigmatism, crime would be simply another occupation.

Concerns over the rights of the individual faced with the power of the state to punish crimes is a prominent feature of the U.S. Constitution, which is also at the heart of how fairly laws are enforced and how impartially justice is meted out.

Sociologists who study crime found that punishment is not clearly connected to deterrence. Researchers have shown that whatever the punishment, a high likelihood of arrest is the greatest deterrent of crime.

Rehabilitation rests on the concept of crime as a social aberration and the offender as a social misfit whose aberrant behavior can be modified to conform to society's norms. Rehabilitation usually includes varying amounts of counseling, educational and training programs, and work experience. There are no guidelines about which form of rehabilitation will work best with a particular kind of offender, as studies of ***recidivism***—the probability that a former innate will break the law after release and be arrested again—have not produced any firm conclusions.

Some of the barriers to effective rehabilitation are the result of bureaucracy and the constraints of prison life that make application difficult. Work release programs in which prisoners are allowed to leave prison for periods of time to work have met with some success.

Crime prevention is defined in three different ways: 1) the sum total of all influences and activities that contribute to the development of a nondeviant personality, 2) attempts to deal with conditions in a person's environment that are believed to lead to crime and delinquency, and 3) specific services or programs designed to prevent further crime and delinquency.

Programs based on the first definition include measures designed to improve the social environment, such as improved housing and job opportunities for ghetto dwellers. These have demonstrated little success. Efforts based on the second definition include efforts to reduce children's exposure to antisocial and/or illegal activities. These have had some notable successes. Most programs work within the third definition. They include approaches such as parole, probation, and training schools. Some experimental programs have demonstrated the feasibility of using untrained youth to develop welfare programs rather than relying on outside professionals.

Social Policy

In their efforts to reduce crime, governments at all levels experience more frustration than success. New kinds of crime are invented, and social change creates changes in the definition of crime. In 2005, the U.S. Supreme Court struck down the federal mandatory sentencing law that required judges to impose specific sentences in criminal cases. Social policies to control crime or punish criminals are not formulated only at the federal level; states and municipalities also promote new policies and approaches.

Even though only a small percentage of criminals are arrested and convicted, the court and prison systems are overloaded. Controversial strategies, like ***plea bargaining***—in which the offender agrees to plead guilty to a lesser charge and free the courts from the need to conduct a jury trial—and experimental techniques, like community corrections, are not reducing the burden.

The prison paradox concerns the fact that as crime rates have decreased over the past few years, rates of imprisonment of Americans have increased. The United States now has the highest imprisonment rate in the world. The racial disparities in sentencing in the United States are dramatic.

The costs of imprisonment are soaring, and community alternatives to incarceration are being sought. The majority of adults in the custody of U.S. correctional systems are under community supervision through probation or parole. ***Probation*** is supervision of offenders who have not been sentenced to jail or prison. ***Parole*** is supervision of people who have been released from prison.

Penalties for occupational and corporate crime are so low that executives and corporations consider the penalties to be acceptable risks. One way to make the risk greater is to increase the fines and penalties. Another approach may be to simplify the laws so that breaking them becomes easier to detect.

Corruption, insulation of top crime executives, and difficulty in obtaining evidence makes it difficult to prosecute organized crime. The FBI, however, has made progress as it has assigned more of its resources to organized crime.

Experts agree that there are too many laws against certain types of juvenile behavior and too many laws against victimless crimes. This makes policy hard to create and administer. Some community-based policies have had success, but at the same time juvenile crimes rates are rising, which creates considerable confusion about public policy toward serious juvenile crime.

There are increasing demands for more gun control, but opponents argue that it is a right guaranteed in the Second Amendment of the Constitution, and there are other ways to kill. Others point out that murder is the result of the impulse to kill, the lethal capacity of the weapon, and the availability of the weapon. Gun control would eliminate the last two. Public opinion about gun control seems to fluctuate with the murder rate. States and municipalities have passed their own laws. In addition to new laws, strategies also include product liability lawsuits against gun manufacturers. Other strategies have focused on detecting and seizing guns in high crime areas.

Going Beyond Left and Right

Liberals believe that crime is caused by social-structural factors, such as poverty, and recommend rehabilitative strategies for offenders. Conservatives stress personal responsibility and the rights of crime victims. Nonetheless, without the rule of law, the distinctions between left and right are absurd.

RESEARCH NAVIGATOR EXERCISES

ContentSelect

Select the criminal justice database and use the keywords *women* and *crime*. Look for articles on domestic violence. Read the June, 2007 article by Gover and her colleagues, entitled "A Specialized Domestic Violence Court in South Carolina." (*AN 25236407*) What is so special about this particular court? What are your impressions in terms of its usefulness?

New York Times Online

Use sociology as the subject and enter the keyword *homicide*. One of the issues targeted in the text is racial disparity in sentencing. Read the 10/7/2007 article "Race Gap: Crime vs. Punishment." What are the major conclusions of this analysis? Do you agree or disagree?

Link Library

Use sociology as the subject. Click on C for crime, then on crime. Look for the Bureau of Justice Statistics. Under Special Topics, find and click on international statistics. Look for the World Fact Book of Criminal Justice Systems. This will take you to the Statistics About page. Next, select one or two developed countries and one or two less developed countries to compare. For example, you could compare Japan and the United States to Kenya and Nigeria. Make a note of some of the differences you observe. Next, return to the Statistics About page, and click on homicide trends in the special topics section. Look at the trends for special groups, e.g., look at the trends in infanticide and eldercide. Describe these trends. Are you surprised at the rates for infants, and who is most likely to kill them? What about the trends for the elderly?

PRACTICE TEST

MULTIPLE CHOICE QUESTIONS: Select the one best answer for each of the following questions.

1. The crime ____ collects data on the most serious and most frequently occurring crimes.
   a. index
   b. scale
   c. monitor
   d. factor

2. According to the FBI Crime Clock, which of the following is true?
   a. Forcible rapes occur more frequently than larceny thefts.
   b. Burglary occurs more frequently than robbery.
   c. Robbery occurs more frequently than burglary.
   d. Aggravated assault occurs more frequently than larceny theft.

3. Which of the following deals with noncriminal acts in which individual injures another?
   a. civil law
   b. criminal law
   c. the Crime Index
   d. victimless crimes

4. _______ is unlawful homicide without malice aforethought.
   a. Murder
   b. Second degree murder
   c. Manslaughter
   d. none of the above

5. What were the names of the two groups in William Chambliss's classic study of middle-class and lower-class boys?
   a. Sharks and Jets
   b. Hoods and Cools
   c. Angels and Devils
   d. Saints and Roughnecks

6. Which of the following is true with respect to murder?
   a. Most murders take place between strangers.
   b. Most murders take place between people who know each other well.
   c. Most murders are carefully planned.
   d. The mentally ill have a much higher rate of committing murder than the general population.

7. Which of the following statements regarding murder is NOT true?
   a. More than half of all murder victims are members of minority groups.
   b. Men are more likely to be murderers than women.
   c. Murder victims tend to be older.
   d. Most of the time, killer and victim are of the same race.

8. Check forgery, vandalism, and shoplifting are classified in the text as:
   a. white collar crimes.
   b. petty crimes.
   c. public order crimes.
   d. occasional property crimes.

9. Prostitution is an example of a _____ crime.
   a. violent
   b. property
   c. victimless
   d. conventional

10. Drug trafficking is an example of:
   a. organized crime.
   b. white-collar crime.
   c. corporate crime.
   d. conventional crime.

11. _________ are dedicated to a life of crime; they live by it and pride themselves on their accomplishments.
   a. Professional criminals
   b. White-collar criminals
   c. Embezzlers
   d. Mass murderers

12. ________ is a crime in which the perpetrator intentionally selects a victim because of the victim's perceived race, color, national origin, ethnicity, gender, disability, or sexual orientation.
   a. Stalking
   b. Hate crime
   c. Institutional discrimination
   d. Racism

13. Running away and vagrancy are examples of which type of crime?
   a. status
   b. conventional
   c. victimless
   d. public order

14. Which of the following countries has the highest death rate from firearms?
   a. Israel
   b. Denmark
   c. Canada
   d. the United States

15. _________ theory argues that crime is learned within the context of small, intimate groups like family and friends.
   a. Anomie
   b. Differential association
   c. Social control
   d. Labeling

16. Differential association is a concept relating to which theory?
   a. functionalism
   b social-conflict
   c. symbolic-interactionism
   d. none of the above

17. According to Walter Miller's classic study of street gangs, which of the following is a focal concern that often leads to the violation of middle class and legal norms?
    a. ambition
    b. academic skills
    c. ability to defer gratification
    d. none of the above

18. Which of the following perspectives on social control assumes that offenders can be cured so that they can conform to society's norms?
    a. retribution
    b. deterrence
    c. rehabilitation
    d. prevention

19. _______ refers to the probability that a former inmate will break the law after release and be arrested again.
    a. Plea bargaining
    b. Incapacitation
    c. Recidivism
    d. Interdiction

20. Which of the following nations has the highest incarceration rate?
    a. the United States
    b. Russia
    c. Sweden
    d. China

ESSAY QUESTIONS

1. Describe the Uniform Crime Report and the National Victimization Survey and discuss potential problems with each.

2. Compare and contrast the various types of crime.

3. Compare and contrast the sociological theories of crime.

4. Critique the biological theories of crime.

5. Identify and discuss the strategies for controlling crime. What difficulties are presented by each approach?

6. Describe the relationship between gender and crime, between race and crime, and between age and crime.

ANSWERS TO MULTIPLE CHOICE QUESTIONS

1.	a	11.	a
2.	b	12.	b
3.	a	13.	a
4.	d	14.	d
5.	c	15.	b
6.	b	16.	c
7.	c	17.	d
8.	a	18.	c
9.	c	19.	c
10.	a	20.	a

CHAPTER SIX

Poverty Amid Affluence

CHAPTER OUTLINE

- I. The Haves and the Have-Nots
  - A. The Rich
    - 1. Are the Rich a Social Problem?
  - B. The Poor
    - 1. The Working Poor
    - 2. The Severely Poor
- II. Poverty and Social Class
- III. The Nature of Poverty
  - A. The Poverty Line
  - B. Who Are the Poor?
    - 1. Poverty and Single-Parent Families
    - 2. Child Poverty and the Frayed U.S. Safety Net
    - 3. Poverty and Minority Groups
    - 4. Poverty and Geography
    - 5. Rural Poverty
    - 6. The Dependent Poor
  - C. Event Poverty
    - 1. Hurricane Katrina: Poverty, Race, and Class
    - 2. Immigration and Poverty
- IV. Concomitants of Poverty
  - A. Health Care
  - B. Education
  - C. Housing and Homelessness
  - D. Justice
- V. Explanations of Persistent Poverty
  - A. Structural Explanations
  - B. Cultural Explanations
- VI. Social Policy
  - A. Reform of "Welfare as We Know It"
  - B. Welfare Policies and Growing Inequality
  - C. Future Prospects
- VII. Going Beyond Left and Right
- VIII. Summary
- IX. Key Terms
- X. Social Problems Online
- XI. Research Navigator

LEARNING OBJECTIVES

After reading Chapter Six you should:

1. Be familiar with the economic differences between the very rich and the very poor.
2. Understand what is meant by social stratification and social class.
3. Know what the poverty line is and how it is used to determine who is poor.
4. Be familiar with who the poor are and factors that may lead to poverty.
5. Understand the concomitants of poverty: health care, education, housing and homelessness, and justice.
6. Be familiar with the 1996 changes in welfare and perceptions of its impact.
7. Understand structural explanations of the persistency of poverty.
8. Understand the "culture of poverty" and criticisms of the concept.

KEY TERMS

welfare state
wealthfare
working poor
social stratification
class stratification
lumpenproletariat

CHAPTER SUMMARY

The Haves and the Have-Nots

The gap between rich and poor is widening. In general, Americans do not object to inequalities in the actual situation of different groups in society and believe that most Americans have the same chance to achieve material well being. Developing policies that address the problems of the poor, however, could be hampered by this ethic of individual success and enrichment.

An important factor in determining an individual's social class is his or her economic wealth, although it is not the sole determinant. It has become difficult to distinguish between working and middle class because the standard of living of working classes has increased as wages and access to education have increased. However, events of recent decades have reversed the trend toward greater affluence for all, and the gap between the poor and the affluent has increased.

Although equality of opportunity is a central value of American society, equality of outcome is not. Americans do not object to inequalities in the actual situation of different groups in society and believe that most Americans have the same chance to achieve material well-being. The affluent live longer, are better educated, and have more influence than the poor.

One percent of all households hold over one-third of all personal wealth; the wealthiest 20 percent earn 50 percent of the income. The United States has a long history of attempting to redistribute wealth. There are three reasons for this: 1) the wealthy get more and can pay more, 2) they have a greater investment in the system and should pay more to maintain it, and 3) some redistribution is fair and just in a democratic society.

The United States is a ***welfare state***, which means that a significant portion of the Gross National Product (GNP) is taken by the state to provide certain minimum levels of social welfare for the poor and others who would not be able to survive under conditions of market competition. It has also been called a

wealthfare state because of subsidies for the rich. Are the rich a social problem? There is evidence of concern that the ethic of individual success and enrichment may hamper efforts to develop new policies to address the problems of poverty.

The situation of the poor, especially those in the lower ranks of the labor force—the ***working poor***, has become worse. There are several reasons for this, including technological changes that eliminate certain kinds of jobs, the reluctance of the middle and upper classes to share wealth, and the general attitudes of Americans toward poverty. Measured in real wages, wages have actually declined for the working poor since the late 1980s. Severely poor people are those who are below 50 percent of the poverty threshold. The number of severely poor is growing rapidly; 43 percent of persons in poverty are severely poor by national standards. Those who are becoming truly poor are increasing at a rate 56 percent higher than the growth rate of new entrants into poverty.

Poverty and Social Class

Social stratification is a pattern in which individuals and groups are assigned to different positions in the social order, positions that enjoy varying amounts of access to desirable goods and services. ***Class stratification*** is the stratification of individuals and groups according to various occupations, incomes, and skills.

Marxists define social class by those who control the means of production, the workers, and the ***lumpenproletaria***t, who are on the fringes of society. In other words, Marxists define social class in economic terms. Weber emphasized the importance of status in defining social class and pointed out that money alone does not define class. Today sociologists use a combination of both by looking at economic class as well as status.

Sociologists also point out that social class has an objective as well as a subjective dimension. People would not necessarily identify themselves as being in the same class as objective measures would put them in. Fewer people identify themselves as poor than is objectively the case.

The Nature of Poverty

A simple definition of poverty is that the poor have less money to spend, and that the money they have buys less. However, this ignores the fact that people may be in poverty relative to their community even though they may be living above subsistence levels. To deal effectively with poverty as a social problem, more precise, scientific definitions are needed.

The U.S. government defines poverty by estimated costs of achieving a minimal level of nutrition. By this definition, about 12.7 percent of the U.S. population is below the poverty line. Some have argued that this definition ignores benefits the poor receive, such as Medicaid, and is therefore an overestimate. Others argue that official numbers do not consider taxes, out of pocket medical expenses, and other factors that lower income; nor are regional variations considered. If these factors are considered, there may actually be more people below the poverty line.

To deal effectively with poverty, it is important to have a generally agreed-upon, scientifically based and specific definition of poverty. The U.S. government has definitions based on the calculation of a minimum family market basket, which is estimated from average food prices. This makes it possible to define who is above or below the poverty line, although there are criticisms about the accuracy of this measure.

Who are the poor? Since the Social Security Act of 1935, the United States has made improvements in reducing poverty. However, other industrialized countries do more to provide public sector help to poor children. The primary cause of poverty in the United States is being born into single-parent families or the break-up of a two-parent family.

In the United States, 17.8 percent of children under age 18 live in poverty, especially those in single-parent households headed by women. Welfare reform has made it more difficult for women as they are required to work or attend training while still meeting the needs of childcare. Absent fathers frequently cannot make court-ordered child support payments, and there is little incentive for them to help with child care in lieu of monetary child support.

Most of the poor are white, but blacks and other minorities are overrepresented. Factors that contribute to this are low wages, discrimination, and educational deficits. Discrimination in housing complicates matters as it cuts access to higher paying jobs and better schools.

Poor women who head households are among those most affected by welfare reform of 1996 and the increased pressure to find work or training. Theoretically, welfare reform was supposed to provide incentives for recipients to seek work and thereby exit the welfare rolls. This has been an increased burden for single mothers who must find ways to provide child care while they are looking for employment or are working.

Additionally, there is regional variation in poverty. Although less visible than urban poverty, over half the poverty occurs in rural and suburban settings. Among the rural poor are migrant farm workers and Native Americans. Many rural poor attempt to find jobs in urban areas, but discover that the problems they had on the countryside are only magnified. About a fifth of all poor live in rural areas and another 30 percent live in suburbs. Poverty in some rural areas is increasing and this is accompanied by the correlates of poverty: infant mortality, family dissolution, out-migration of the younger and better educated, and malnutrition.

Many of the poor are not responsible for their situation and must turn to public assistance; these are the dependent poor. The mentally retarded represent the highest proportion. The poor are also the victims of myths and misconceptions like the following: The vast majority of the poor are poor because they do not want to work. Poor families are trapped in a cycle of poverty that few escape. Welfare programs for the poor are straining the federal budget. The majority of the poor live in inner-city neighborhoods. The poor live off government welfare. Most of the poor are single mothers and their children.

Many studies show that the poor strongly share the work ethic and regret being on welfare. The largest difference is that they lack confidence in their ability to succeed. They also have limited skills, which makes it difficult to compete in the job market. Even families with two working parents making minimum wages could suddenly drop below the poverty line if an event such as pregnancy, illness, or the loss of one of the jobs occurs (this is known as event poverty). Hurricane Katrina clearly illustrates how an event can very suddenly thrust significant numbers of people into poverty

In wealthier nations, such as the United States, an increasing proportion of the poor are immigrants. Although the majority of Hispanics are neither impoverished nor immigrants, poor people from Mexico, Central America, and the Caribbean are among the largest immigrant groups today.

The issue of whether poor people and unskilled immigrants drive down the wages of the working poor and represent a burden to taxpayers generates a great deal of controversy. However, a study by the National Academy of Sciences showed that economic impact from immigrant workers was beneficial for the economy in general, but did affect the wages of high school dropouts.

Concomitants of Poverty

Most Americans take for granted good health care, decent education and housing, and fair treatment under the law. This section examines the impact of poverty in each of these areas.

The poor are less healthy than the rest of the population. This is true not only of physical health, but mental health as well. Moreover, the poor are less likely to have health insurance, and they are less likely to recognize symptoms of illness. Consequently, they are more likely to put off treatment until illnesses become serious.

Medicare and Medicaid have improved access to health care for the poor, but like most insurance programs, coverage is inadequate. Other government programs are helping somewhat, but none is addressing the overall health problems of the poor, who are victims of malnutrition, higher rates of disease, inadequate housing, sanitation, and rodent control.

In every respect poor children get less education than those born into more affluent families. They receive fewer years of schooling, have less chance of graduating from high school, are much less likely to go to college. They are apt to be taught in overcrowded classrooms, often by inexperienced teachers, and to receive little if any individual attention. Moreover, most teachers come from a middle-class background and have little training in working with disadvantaged children. Studies have shown that preschool helps. Another factor is maternal welfare status. Some evidence suggests that children improve educationally when their mothers move off welfare.

The poor are likely to live in housing that is overcrowded, infested with vermin, in need of major repairs, lacking basic plumbing facilities, and inadequately heated. More than half such housing is in rural areas. Racial segregation and zoning restrictions designed to increase revenue for an area often lead to further low-income housing shortages.

It is difficult to count the number of homeless, but there have been recent attempts to fill knowledge gaps about them through surveys conducted in soup kitchens, shelters, and other programs. One notable finding is the disproportionate number of African-American men among homeless. Another finding is that the majority of homeless had worked for pay in the past month.

Poor people are more likely to be arrested, indicted, convicted, and imprisoned, and are more likely to be given long sentences. They are also less likely to receive probation, parole, or suspended sentences. Because of their situation, the poor are more likely to commit crimes that society is most disapproving of (property theft and assault) and have less access to legal defense.

Explanations of Poverty

Structural explanations attribute poverty to the functioning of dominant institutions of society, such as markets and corporations. When these social structures change, conflicts arise as large numbers of people attempt to adjust to new conditions and new forms of social institutions. This creates a class of people who lack necessary skills or resources and must compete for low-paying jobs. Marxists argue that this creates a reserve army of unemployed that drives down wages for all workers.

Contemporary social scientists may not agree with Marx's theory, but they tend to agree that changes in macro social patterns of growth have a lot to do with increasing poverty. Some have pointed out, for example, that the rapid period of industrialization in the last century reduced poverty by increasing employment and providing the revenue needed to invest in education, housing, jobs, and greater income security for the elderly. Others have pointed out that there are dual labor markets in which some segments of society are given better access to jobs while others are shunted into another segment of the labor market in which jobs pay poorly and offer no security.

Still another structural explanation maintains that the state, through its efforts to eliminate poverty, actually causes it. Radicals argue that state welfare provides enough assistance to keep the poor from challenging the existing capitalist order. Conservatives argue that it takes away incentives for the poor to improve.

Proponents of the cultural approach argue that a culture of poverty arises among people who experience extended periods of economic deprivation. Under these conditions, new norms, values, and aspirations emerge and eventually become independent of the situations that produce them, so that eliminating the problem does not eliminate the behaviors that develop to deal with it. The result is a self-sustaining system of values and behaviors that is handed down from one generation to the next.

Critics of the culture of poverty explanation believe that it is a global label that does not fit all instances. Other factors, like feelings of despair, may explain some of the behavior of the poor. Others point out the heterogeneity of the poor that a global cultural explanation does not address.

Social Policy

Welfare reform of 1996 changed the work requirement for people receiving welfare payments. After two years they must look for work and their eligibility is limited to five years. Conservatives tend to support the changes and argue that it has provided incentives for recipients to work; it has, as a result, built their self-esteem, and it has supported traditional family values, Liberal critics argue that the new system is increasing the number of homeless people and people who lack health insurance, and that it is, in effect, a form of government enforcement of underpaid work.

It is difficult to evaluate where the truth lies because each state and the District of Columbia all have different programs. Consequently, it is difficult to compare the complexity of factors that could be impacting results. It is important, therefore, for social scientists to conduct politically neutral analyses of the empirical facts.

Researchers have noted that countries that rely least on public assistance emphasize such policies as family and housing allowances, child-care services, and various types of work incentives. These employment policies make it easier for adults to manage their work and family lives without undue strain on themselves and their children. One suggested approach to help minimum wage workers is to expand the earned income tax credit so that poor families could get a payment from the IRS, thus creating a negative income tax for the poor.

A policy innovation that holds some promise is a set of experimental programs designed to move people from areas of concentrated poverty to communities where they will have more opportunity. These experiments are showing some success, but it is unclear whether they will ultimately work and receive legislative support.

Going Beyond Left and Right

Critics from both the left and the right agree that welfare programs should encourage people to seek training and employment. Training programs, however, require state and federal funding, child-care support, and jobs for people to fill. These problems make the issue of welfare and work an ongoing challenge to policy makers.

RESEARCH NAVIGATOR EXERCISES

ContentSelect

Select the sociology database. Use *poverty* as the keyword. Read the 7/23/07 article by Carolyn O'Hara entitled, "Escaping the Poverty Trap" (*AN 25803704*). What IS the "poverty trap"? How does O'Hara suggest that the "trap can be escaped"?

New York Times Online

Use sociology as the subject and enter *poverty* as the keyword. Read the 8/7/07 article "The Dusty Archives: A Theory of Affluence." As pointed out in this article, for thousands of years, most of the people of the world lived in abject poverty. When industrialization took place, affluence was born and things changed. Describe this change process. Do you agree or disagree with this "theory" of affluence?

Link Library

Use sociology as the subject. Click on P for poverty. Look at the article Poverty Rate Fails to Decline, as well as poverty statistics, and children in poverty. Examine the information on how the Census Bureau defines poverty; also look at current poverty thresholds. Based on your reading of this information, why do you think children are being dropped from Medicaid even though they are eligible for these benefits? What consequences do you think this will have for the children and their families? Do you think that the poverty definition used by the Census Bureau should be changed? If so, what would you use to recalculate poverty rates? What would the economic impact of this change be?

PRACTICE TEST

MULTIPLE CHOICE QUESTIONS: Select the one best answer for each of the following questions.

1. The median household income in the United States today is approximately
   a. $46,000.
   b. $12,000.
   c. $27,000.
   d. $63,000.

2. The wealthiest 20 percent receive ____ percent of the income.
   a. 20
   b. 30
   c. 40
   d. 50

3. Because the United States uses a significant portion of the GNP to help the poor, aged, and disabled, it is known as a
   a. welfare state.
   b. wealthfare state.
   c. democratic state.
   d. socialist state.

4. Sometimes the United States is know as a wealthfare state because
   a. of high taxes.
   b. of subsidies for the rich.
   c. even the poor are better off than the poor in Third World countries.
   d. the wealthy subsidize the poor.

5. Real wages since the late 1980s have
   a. declined.
   b. improved.
   c. stayed the same.
   d. are no longer a relevant measure.

6. Marxists define social class in ____ terms.
   a. economic
   b. status
   c. revolutionary
   d. political

7. Victor Fuchs proposed that any family may be classified as poor if its income is less than half the median family income. This reflects which view of poverty?
   a. relative
   b. absolute
   c. fluctuating
   d. reactive

8. Of all the children under the age of 18, ____ percent are living in poverty.
   a. 2.3
   b. 17.8
   c. 35.3
   d. 49.3

9. Severe poverty is defined by the Census Bureau as
   a. persons whose family incomes are less than half the official poverty line.
   b. persons whose families rely totally on government subsides.
   c. persons whose families have no adult breadwinner.
   d. persons whose health is at immediate risk due to lack of material and social resources.

10. Much of the recent increase in severe poverty seems to be due to
   a. a new fatalism among the poor.
   b. changes in the definition of severe poverty.
   c. a decrease in subsidies for low-income children and their mothers.
   d. lower divorce rates among the poor.

11. The largest group of poor families are
   a. white.
   b. black.
   c. other minorities.
   d. single men.

12. A significant proportion of the dependent poor are people who
   a. avoid work.
   b. file fraudulent welfare claims.
   c. are disabled.
   d. have given up looking for employment.

13. Poverty resulting from the loss of a job, marital discord, or pregnancy is known as
   a. domestic poverty.
   b. stress poverty.
   c. event poverty.
   d. structural poverty.

14. A study by the National Academy of Science concluded that increased labor supply and the lower prices as a result of immigration
   a. resulted in the loss of 1.5 million jobs.
   b. produced a healthier economy.
   c. had a minimal impact on the economy.
   d. lowered the standard of living for most Americans.

15. Relative to the rest of the population, the poor
   a. have better access to health care.
   b. have the same level of health.
   c. are healthier.
   d. are less healthy.

16. Poor children
   a. receive fewer years of schooling.
   b. have less chance of graduating from high school.
   c. are less likely to go to college.
   d. all of the above

17. One notable finding from a survey by U.S. Department of Housing and Urban Development is that a disproportionate number of _____ are among the homeless.
   a. teenage mothers
   b. African-American men
   c. elderly women
   d. white men

18. Poor people are more likely to be
   a. arrested.
   b. convicted.
   c. imprisoned.
   d. all of the above

19. Which of the following appears to fault poor people the most for their poverty?
   a. the Marxian view
   b. structural views
   c. the culture of poverty
   d. the situational approach

20. One of the most difficult problems in attempting to improve the conditions of the poor is
   a. trying to motivate them to work.
   b. funding enough day-care centers.
   c. what to do about people living in highly concentrated or segregated poor neighborhoods.
   d. getting them into college.

ESSAY QUESTIONS

1. What do the authors mean when they state that equality of opportunity is basic to American ideals but the equality of outcome is not?

2. Define and distinguish social stratification and social class.

3. Discuss the nature of poverty. What is the poverty line? How is it calculated? Is the method of calculation a valid one?

4. List and describe the concomitants of poverty.

5. Discuss what is meant by the "culture of poverty" and some of the criticisms of the concept.

ANSWERS TO MULTIPLE CHOICE QUESTIONS

1.	a	11.	a
2.	d	12.	c
3.	a	13.	c
4.	b	14.	b
5.	a	15.	d
6.	a	16.	d
7.	a	17.	b
8.	b	18.	d
9.	a	19.	c
10.	c	20.	c

CHAPTER SEVEN

Racism, Prejudice, and Discrimination

CHAPTER OUTLINE

I. The Continuing Struggle for Minority Civil Rights
II. The Social Construction of Minorities
III. Defining Racism, Prejudice, and Discrimination
IV. Origins of Prejudice and Discrimination
  A. Prejudice and Bigotry in the Individual
    1. Frustration-Aggression
    2. Projection
  B. Prejudice and Bigotry in Social Structures
  C. Cultural Factors: Norms and Stereotypes
    1. Social Norms
    2. Stereotyping
V. Institutional Discrimination
    1. Racial Profiling
  A. Education
    1. Unequal Access to High-Quality Schooling
  B. Housing
  C. Employment and Income
  D. Justice
    1. Imprisonment and Employment Discrimination
    2. Racial Inequalities in Capital Punishment
  E. Political Discrimination
    1. Felony Disenfranchisement
    2. Anti-Voter Fraud Campaigns
VI. Some Consequences of Prejudice and Discrimination
VII. Social Policy
  A. Job Training
  B. Affirmative Action
  C. Education for Equality
  D. Future Prospects
VII. Going Beyond Left and Right
VIII. Summary
IX. Key Terms
X. Social Problems Online
XI. Research Navigator

LEARNING OBJECTIVES

After reading Chapter Seven you should:

1. Know what is meant by being a minority and be able to define key terms associated with prejudice and discrimination.

2. Discuss the impact of prejudice and discrimination on individual minority members.
3. Be prepared to compare and contrast frustration-aggression explanations of prejudice and discrimination from projection explanations.
4. Identify social and cultural factors that have been used to explain prejudice and discrimination.
5. Be prepared to discuss the impact of institutional discrimination on education.
6. Be prepared to discuss the impact of institutional discrimination on housing.
7. Be prepared to discuss the impact of institutional discrimination on employment and income.
8. Be prepared to discuss the impact of institutional discrimination on the criminal justice system.
9. Discuss reactions to affirmative action and potential alternatives.
10. Discuss Head Start and its effectiveness in early intervention.

KEY TERMS

racial minorities
ethnic minorities
assimilation
endogamy
racism
discrimination
prejudice
scapegoat
projection
social norm
homogamy
stereotyping
institutional discrimination
de jure segregation
de facto segregation
racial steering
affirmative action
Head Start

CHAPTER SUMMARY

The Continuing Struggle for Minority Rights

Although the constitutional bases for racial equality were established in the 1860s and 1870s with the ratification of the Thirteenth, Fourteenth, and Fifteenth Amendments, it was not until the mid-twentieth century that the rights guaranteed by these amendments began to be exercised effectively. A major legal breakthrough came in 1954 with the historic decision in *Brown v. Board of Education of Topeka* that "separate educational facilities are inherently unequal." Still, the discrepancy between legal equality and actual inequality remains. In 1968, the National Advisory Commission on Civil Disorders concluded that "our nation is moving toward two societies, one black, one white—separate and unequal."

The Social Construction of Minorities

The most significant minorities are those that do not receive the same treatment as other groups in society. Three concepts help us to understand how this can come about: racial minorities, ethnic minorities, and assimilation.

Racial minorities are groups of people who share certain inherited characteristics, such as eye folds or brown skin. ***Ethnic minorities*** consist of people who share cultural features, such as language, religion, national origin, dietary practices, and a common history, and who regard themselves as a common group. When members of either a racial or an ethnic minority take on the characteristics of the mainstream culture by adapting their own unique cultural patterns to those of the majority, as well as intermarrying, ***assimilation*** occurs.

Some sociologically significant attributes of minorities are that they are subordinate social segments, they have special physical or cultural traits that are seen as undesirable, they have a group consciousness, membership is transmitted by a rule of descent, and they tend to practice ***endogamy***, marriage within the group.

There is really a continuum from dominant to minority, and different groups move along the continuum at various times. It is usually more difficult for racial groups with distinctive racial characteristics to move toward dominance and thus they tend to remain minorities for longer periods. It is also possible to put nonracial or nonethnic groups, like the aged or homosexuals, on this continuum. Finally, it should be pointed out that the dominant group is not always the most numerous; it must merely be able to prevent other groups from effectively challenging its power.

Defining Racism, Prejudice, and Discrimination

Racism is behavior, in word or deed, which is motivated by the belief that human races have distinctive characteristics that determine abilities and cultures. Racists believe in the erroneous concept of race; they also believe that their own race is superior and therefore ought to dominate. Discrimination is the differential treatment of individuals considered to belong to a particular social group; it is always overt, but may be difficult to observe. Sometimes people rationalize discrimination on the grounds that the minority groups are less worthy. In addition, people tend to be ethnocentric and see their own behavioral patterns and belief structures as desirable and natural and those of others as less so. Rationalization and ethnocentricity lead to prejudice, which is a rigid emotional attitude against members of the subordinate group.

Discrimination is behavior whereas prejudice is attitude. ***Prejudice*** is an emotional or rigid attitude against members of a subordinate group. Robert Merton identified four relationships among them: unprejudiced and nondiscriminatory (integration), unprejudiced and discriminatory (institutional discrimination), prejudiced and nondiscriminatory (latent bigotry), and prejudiced and discriminatory (outright bigotry). **Table 7-1** illustrates Merton's typology.

Origins of Prejudice and Discrimination

The origins of prejudice and discrimination are numerous and complex and can partly be found in individual attitudes and behaviors and partly in the structural organization of society. ***Frustration-aggression*** theory suggests to us that sometimes humans feel frustrated at an inability to get something they want; this can lead to aggression, which is sometimes displaced towards a ***scapegoat*** rather than the real cause of the aggression. When this displacement is not limited to a particular person but is extended to include all similar people, it may produce a more or less permanent prejudice.

When people possess undesirable traits that they cannot rid themselves of, they project those onto members of another group. This makes it possible for them to reject and condemn the traits without rejecting and condemning themselves. This is known as ***projection***.

Prejudice and bigotry are also built into social structures. In many societies the demand for more than the available supply of certain goods gives rise to a competitive struggle, which usually results in the dominance of one group by another. Economic exploitation is one form of discrimination practiced by the dominant group to keep the subordinate group subordinate. This discrimination can be practical, such as legal restrictions, or it can be symbolic, such as refusing service to certain racial groups.

Cultural factors are also involved. A ***social norm*** is a commonly accepted standard that specifies the kind of behavior appropriate in a given situation. A good example of a social norm that pertains to minority-majority relations is ***homogamy***, the requirement that one must marry a person similar to oneself in religion, social class, and race or ethnicity. Recent research shows that the norm of homogamy is far weaker today than it was 20 years ago.

Stereotyping is not confined to any particular group, nor is it unique to the United States. Still another source of prejudice and discrimination is ***stereotyping***, or attributing a fixed and usually unfavorable or inaccurate conception to a category of people.

Institutional Discrimination

Sometimes, discrimination becomes built into the social structure of a society and is not the result of the conscious prejudice of individuals. When this occurs, discrimination becomes institutional. In the United States this has occurred in education, housing, employment and income, and in the criminal justice system. When discrimination is an unconscious result of the structure and function of public institutions and policies, rather than conscious prejudices of public officials, it is ***institutional discrimination***.

Because of institutional discrimination, minorities have less access to quality income, tend to be segregated in housing and education, and experience fewer opportunities for higher income employment. Furthermore, minorities are more likely to be arrested, convicted, and serve longer sentences than nonminorities.

If discrimination is a socially learned behavior of members of dominant groups, designed to support and justify their continued dominance, it is reasonable that it will be built into the structure of society. ***Racial profiling*** refers to the practice by law enforcement personnel, security agents, or any person in a position of authority to disproportionately selecting people of color for investigations or other forms of discrimination, which often includes invasion of privacy.

Conservatives argue that racial profiling is justified because facts support that some races are more likely to commit crimes; others argue that it is a violation of civil rights and is a form of institutional discrimination.

Since the 1940 census, the average number of years of school completed by all Americans has increased steadily. Despite these gains, however, members of minority groups still have less chance of finishing high school or attending college than do whites. Recent studies have found that the level of education of one's parents and their net worth are the two best predictors of the quality of higher education their children will receive. Although African Americans are finishing high school at higher rates, because their parents have relatively less wealth they are unable to achieve quality higher education.

Brown v. the Board of Education of Topeka affirmed that separate schooling was not equal, which effectively wiped out ***de jure segregation***, or discrimination required by law. But states and municipalities also had to address ***de facto segregation***, which results from housing patterns, economic inequalities, gerrymandered school districts, and the departure of middle-class families from communities with increasing rates of minority households and poor or mediocre schools. This was attempted through busing, which is considered a failure today. No alternative strategies have been suggested and funding has not met the increased demand for better schools in lower-income minority neighborhoods.

A study by the Harvard Project on School Desegregation found that resegregation of the races is increasing. This is true despite the growing diversity of minority enrollments as a result of recent immigration.

Housing segregation has diminished somewhat in recent years as a result of immigration into formerly segregated neighborhoods, but it remains a serious obstacle to the achievement of racial and ethnic harmony. Studies have shown that failure to enforce federal laws against housing discrimination continues to produce rates of black segregation that are far higher than those experienced by any other group in U.S. history.

A practice that contributes to high rates of segregation is racial steering, in which real estate brokers refuse to show houses outside of specific areas to minority buyers, despite the fact that restrictive covenants against minorities are illegal. Housing problems of Native Americans provide further examples of how segregation and faulty application of social policies worsen an already difficult situation.

Discrimination is no less prevalent in employment that it is in education and housing. In some ways discrimination in employment is a direct result of discrimination in education, since education is directly related to income and employment.

One possible solution is apprenticeships and training through labor unions. However, labor unions, despite the rhetoric of their leadership and established policies, have resisted internal changes or economic sacrifices to accommodate the demands of minority workers.

Although there has been some improvement on income equality, it is also important to look at asset equality. Minorities tend to own fewer assets, which has an intergenerational impact since those who don't own assets have nothing to pass to their children.

As manufacturing jobs disappear, education becomes an important means by which minorities can get jobs. However, inadequate schools and increased isolation of black and Latinos make it difficult to learn the skills and mannerisms of the dominant white middle class. Consequently, many employers have had negative experiences with African Americans, especially young men, and tend to be wary of employing them. **Tables 7-2** through **7-4** show evidence of the inequalities between blacks and whites in terms of housing, income, and education.

The American justice system is based on two assumptions: 1) justice is blind, and 2) an accused person is considered innocent until proven guilty. These two assumptions do not seem to be applied equally. Considerable evidence exists that discrimination plays a role in who is arrested, in who gets bail, and in sentencing. All black males who seek employment are subject to racial discrimination, but black men who serve in prison are even more likely to be discriminated against in the job market.

There is evidence that there is discrimination in capital crimes, although receiving the death sentence appears to be based more on the race of the victim than the race of the accused.

Members of minority groups are systematically courted by politicians for their votes, but at the same time, patterns of political discrimination can be found throughout the United States.

In many states, people convicted of a felony may lose the right to vote: This is known as *felony disenfranchisement.*

Civil rights groups note that recent state and federal efforts to investigate voter fraud and institute new systems of voter identification can be seen as attempts to block higher minority voter turnouts.

Some Consequences of Prejudice and Discrimination

The consequences of discrimination and prejudice are both individual and social. Prejudice impacts individual minority members' self-esteem, for example, but it also can lead to violence and aggression directed at minorities. Institutional discrimination and its accompanying prejudice affect the individual personalities of minority group members. Both individuals and groups develop protective reactions against prejudice and discrimination.

There is evidence that both minority children and white children form negative views of minority children as a result of prejudice and discrimination. However, with continuing friendly contact, these prejudices can be broken down and even change their parents' attitudes.

The most common reaction against inequality during the past few decades has been public protest. Such protests produced some success, but as economic and political conditions changed they become less effective. Some have argued that welfare rolls were increased in response to protests and riots and that this had the effect of mollifying blacks.

Upper-class blacks often experience prejudice that is considerably more subtle and more difficult to confront, such as patronizing comments, lack of service, verbal epithets and public harassment, and other threats. Research has suggested, however, that blacks are increasingly willing to assert their rights even in embarrassing public situations and are demanding redress.

The consequences of prejudice can also be seen in the events following the collapse of communism, the easing of the Cold War, and the rise of anti-Western terrorism. Rising nationalism and growing tensions has led to an increase in outbreaks of violence and turf defense where minorities are attacked for being in white areas.

Social Policy

Race continues to be an important factor in American politics. Initially after the Civil War, northerners and African Americans tended to vote for Republicans and southerners for Democrats. This trend has reversed, however, as Democrats tended to support programs that addressed the effects of prejudice and discrimination (e.g., job training).

Federal and state policies and programs have attempted to redress past discrimination, but are met with controversy. Affirmative action programs, for example, are sometimes criticized as being reverse discrimination. However, attempts at eliminating affirmative action have resulted in less access to quality colleges and universities for minorities. Other solutions are being proposed and tested, but some argue that a redistribution of wealth and power is required.

Political demands to reduce taxes reduced training and employment programs. Corporate downsizing has resulted in more qualified workers competing with less well-trained workers. Minorities tend to suffer most from these trends.

Affirmative action is a policy designed to redress past institutional discrimination. Because the policy attempted to motivate organizations to give minorities more opportunities, it is viewed by some as reverse discrimination. Admissions to colleges and professional schools have become a key focus for legal actions that oppose affirmative action. Many states have begun to dismantle their affirmative action programs, but have seen precipitous drops in minority enrollments, especially California. Some corporations continue affirmative action programs because they don't want to alienate their customers, especially those operating in global markets.

In addition to affirmative action, there are other ways to address past discriminations. For example, southern African-American farms have successfully sued the federal government for past discrimination in farm loans. However, analysis of employment data show that even at exactly the same levels of education and training and even with the same college grade point averages, white male college graduates earn 10 to 15 percent more than comparable female, black male, or Asian male graduates.

Studies have shown that native-born blacks are still the most racially segregated group in America. The lack of vigorous enforcement of antidiscrimination legislation is resulting in the reversal of a twenty-year trend in decreasing segregation in schools. Recognition of this is likely to spur efforts to increase funding for preschool programs that address the needs of children in communities where segregation and discrimination have produced persistent rates of school failure. These are known as ***Head Start programs***.

There are some basic flaws in Head Start. Although programs are based on early intervention, there are few guidelines about what that means. It is also argued that Head Start does too little, too late to be effective. Funding for such programs is insufficient to provide quality training and sufficient compensation to retain effective people. More affluent people are increasingly putting their children in preschool programs that are better than the Head Start programs.

Most experts agree that minorities will have to continually struggle to hold on to past gains in the face of increased racism in American society. Government jobs, which make up a sizable portion of minority employment opportunities are diminishing. In the private sector, monitoring of employment trends is decreasing, which makes it harder to combat discrimination.

Bilingual education is increasingly under attack. Social welfare programs for Native Americans are declining. There's a trend for minority groups to emphasize their cultural identity. Critics argue that this could lead to increased segregation unless there is redistribution of wealth and power.

Going Beyond Left and Right

Conservatives tend to dislike affirmative action because it often discriminates against individuals who themselves are not responsible for past patterns of racism and discrimination. Liberals want to redress old patterns of racism and discrimination. William J. Wilson and others argue for race-blind social policies that will not create reverse discrimination but will address past patterns of racism and inequality.

RESEARCH NAVIGATOR EXERCISES

ContentSelect
Select the sociology database and enter the keywords *environmental racism*. This concept refers to the fact that persons of color are more likely to be subjected to pollution, toxins, and other environmental risks than are whites. Explore articles that look at this phenomenon. An example is "Environmental Racism: Smoke and Figures" (2/15/2007 - *AN 24164162*).

New York Times Online
Use the keyword *racism*. One of the articles you will find is Richard Sandomir and Michael Schmidt's "Sharpton Seeks an Apology over Thomas's Language." (10/07/2007), which explores the comment that Isaiah Thomas made in a deposition concerning sexual harassment charges – to wit: that it is less offensive for a black man to refer to a black woman as a "bitch" in comparison with a white man. Sharpton has demanded an apology. What are your reactions to sports figures who are charged with sexual harassment? Should these people be held more accountable for their actions? By whom?

Link Library
Use sociology as the subject. Click on R for racism. Next, click on the Southern Poverty Law Center. At the top of their Web page, note how individual and structural racism are defined. Try to think of examples of each. Next, on this page, click on Tolerance.org. Look for the Dig Deeper section. Click first on Hidden Bias. You will find tests for bias against a number of groups including Native Americans, Blacks, Arabs/Muslims, the elderly, the obese, the gay/homosexual, as well as tests for skin tone preference. Take several of these tests to see how you use stereotypes and bias. Next, return to the Tolerance.org page and the Dig Deeper section. Click on ways to deconstruct language. Review this information. Do you use language in an unbiased or biased way? Return to Tolerance.org and the Dig Deeper section, and click on hidden history. Had you ever heard of any of the history listed in this site? Why or why not? Were you surprised? Finally, consider to what extent selective presentation of history, socialization, and language bias plays a role in individual and structural racism.

PRACTICE QUESTIONS

MULTIPLE CHOICE QUESTIONS: Select the one best answer for each of the following questions.

1. When members of a racial or an ethnic minority take on the characteristics of the mainstream culture by adapting their own unique cultural patterns to those of the majority, _______ occurs.
   a. assimilation c. segregation
   b. integration d. equality

2. Marriage within a group is known as
   a. exogamy. c. endogamy.
   b. monogamy. d. incest.

3. Discrimination is _____ behavior.
   a. covert c. unseen
   b. overt d. implicit

4. _______ is an attitude; it is a tendency to think about people in a categorical, predetermined way.
   a. Racism c. Prejudice
   b. Discrimination d. Bigotry

5. A _________ is a commonly accepted standard that specifies the kind of behavior that is appropriate in a given situation.

a.	social norm	c.	stereotype
b.	law	d.	prejudice

6. A _________ is a fixed and usually unfavorable or inaccurate conception of a category of people.

a.	social norm	c.	stereotype
b.	law	d.	prejudice

7. _________ is the practice by law enforcement personnel, security agents, or any person in a position of authority of disproportionately selecting people of color for investigations.

a.	Stereotyping	c.	Endogamy
b.	Racial profiling	d.	Social norming

8. Segregation resulting from housing patterns, economic inequalities, gerrymandered school districts, and the departure of middle-class families from communities with increasing rates of minority households and poor or mediocre schools is known as
   a. de jure segregation.
   b. de facto segregation.
   c. ipso facto segregation.
   d. discrimination.

9. ______ occurs when real estate brokers refuse to show houses outside of specific areas to minority buyers.
   a. Racial profiling
   b. Racial steering
   c. De jure segregation
   d. De facto segregation

10. Discrimination in employment is a direct result of discrimination
    a. in education.
    b. in housing.
    c. by financial institutions.
    d. by the legal system.

11. In capital crimes, minority offenders would more likely
    a. be acquitted.
    b. receive the death penalty.
    c. receive legal assistance.
    d. none of the above

12. In many states, people convicted of a felony may lose the right to vote. This is known as
    a. felony disenfranchisement.
    b. discrimination.
    c. nonaffirmative action.
    d. racial profiling

13. The most common reaction against inequality during the past few decades has been
    a. violence.
    b. passive resistance.
    c. public protest.
    d. ignoring the issue.

14. _________ refers to policies based on a body of federal law originating in the 1964 Civil Rights Act that bans discrimination on the basis of race, religion, sex, or national origin in such areas as employment, education, and housing.
    a. Job training
    b. Affirmative action
    c. Constitutional convention
    d. Apartheid

15. The passage of the Civil Rights Act of ____ changed the pattern of voting in the South from the Democrats and toward the Republicans.
    a. 1920 c. 1964
    b. 1935 d. 1976

16. In California, Proposition 209
    a. ended affirmative action programs in public college admissions and in government hiring and contracts.
    b. made redlining illegal.
    c. provided funding for minority job training programs.
    d. none of the above

17. The Harvard Project on School Desegregation found that
    a. desegregation of the races is increasing.
    b. resegregation of the races is increasing.
    c. while the South is resegregating, the other regions of the country are not.
    d. there has been no change with respect to desegregation of the races.

18. __________ is a blanket term that refers to federally funded preschool programs aimed at preparing disadvantaged children for school.
    a. Desegregation
    b. Reverse discrimination
    c. Head Start
    d. Redlining

19. In response to attacks on affirmative action, school desegregation, and many other policies designed to integrate American society, minority groups are increasingly developing a form of "_____ politics."
    a. residual
    b. identity
    c. ritual
    d. retreatist

20. William J. Wilson argues for what kind of policies to address past patterns of racism?
   a. reverse discrimination
   b. quotas
   c. race-blind policies
   d. none of the above

ESSAY QUESTIONS

1. Explain the concept of minority group.

2. Distinguish between prejudice and discrimination and discuss their origins.

3. Explain what is meant by institutional discrimination and show how it affects education, housing, employment, and justice.

4. Describe the consequences of discrimination for both the dominant and subordinate group.

5. Discuss the role of federal and state policies and programs in reducing discrimination, for example, affirmative action and Head Start.

ANSWERS TO MULTIPLE CHOICE QUESTIONS

1.	a	11.	b
2.	c	12.	a
3.	b	13.	c
4.	c	14.	b
5.	a	15.	c
6.	c	16.	a
7.	b	17.	b
8.	b	18.	c
9.	b	19.	b
10.	a	20.	c

CHAPTER EIGHT

Gender and Sexuality

CHAPTER OUTLINE

I. Traditional Sex Roles
II. Gender Identity and Sexual Orientation
  A. Gender versus Sexual Identity
  B. Homosexuality
    1. Social-Scientific Perspectives on Sexual Orientation
    2. Who Becomes Gay or Lesbian?
    3. Lesbianism
    4. The Gay Subculture
III. Sexism and Gender Inequality
  A. Power and Male Hegemony
  B. Stereotyping
  C. Sexism and Employment
    1. Unequal Pay for Equal Work
    2. For Minority Women, an Even Wider Wage Gap
  D. Sexual Harassment
  E. Homemaking
IV. Sources of Sexism
  A. Socialization
  B. Education
  C. The Family
  D. Language and the Media
  E. Organized Religion
  F. Government
  G. The Legal System
V. Sources of Homophobia
VI. Social Policy
  A. The Women's Movement
  B. Changes in Child-Rearing Practices
  C. Changes in the Educational System
  D. Changes in the Legal System
  E. Reproductive Control
  F. Changes n Men's Roles
  G. Gay Rights
  H. Future Prospects
VII. Going Beyond Left and Right
VII. Summary
VIII. Key Terms
IX. Social Problems Online
X. Research Navigator

LEARNING OBJECTIVES

After reading Chapter Eight you should:

1. Understand the traditional sex role and the double standard.
2. Be able to distinguish gender roles from sex roles and explain the differences.
3. Know the impact of sexism on career choices and wage differences that men and women experience.
4. Be familiar with sources of sexism, including socialization, education, language, family, organized religion, government, and the legal system.
5. Be familiar with explanations for the sources of homosexuality.
6. Explain why homosexuality is difficult to study.
7. Understand socialization in relationship to sexism and sexual inequality.
8. Know the important policy issues that are being confronted by the women's movement and the gay rights movement.

KEY TERMS

gender identity
sexual identity
homosexuality
sexism
sexual harassment
socialization
homophobia
comparable worth

CHAPTER SUMMARY

Traditional Sex Roles

Until fairly recently it was widely accepted that the only desirable roles for a woman were wife, mother, and homemaker, and that her entire life should revolve around them. These roles emphasized nurturing and skill at emotional aspects of relationships. By contrast, men's roles required them to be leaders, providers, and highly rational and unemotional. The entire range of social norms and values reflected different standards of behavior for men and women.

This double standard is not unique to the United States. In many Latin American and Muslim countries, the status of women is far more subordinate than in the United States. The traditional hierarchy is extremely resistant to change. Women and men are shaped by the culture in which they are raised, so that most adults are thoroughly indoctrinated or socialized for the roles their culture has prescribed from them.

Change is suspect and threatens identity. It is clear, however, that behavioral differences between men and women are learned, and there are considerable differences across societies between what is considered masculine and feminine behavior.

Gender Identity and Sexual Identity

Gender and sexual identity are distinct concepts; one's identity of being male or female is distinct from the sense of one's attractiveness to others and comfort with one's body and feelings of sexual arousal. There is not a binary distinction between male and female either in their gender identity or sexual identity. ***Gender identity***, a sense of maleness or femaleness, is an important part of self-identity. It is typically formed by the age of 3, and by adolescence one's self-identity can range from self-confidence about gender roles to feeling conflicted.

Sexual identity is the sense of one's attractiveness to others and comfort with one's body and feelings of sexual arousal. It also is developed by adolescence and includes *sexual orientation,* or whether one is attracted to members of the opposite sex (heterosexual) or to members of the same sex (homosexual), and *sexuality*, or how one behaves sexually.

There is wide variation in sexual attitudes, behaviors, and lifestyles due to the biological and social forces that shape sexuality. *Transgendered* and *intersexual* individuals, for example, are a diverse group that includes people who feel a strong identification with the other gender; people who cross-dress occasionally or regularly, and people who actually change their bodies through the use of hormones and surgery. Human sexual development is never complete; it is a continuous process that begins at conception and ends at death.

Homosexuality is a sexual preference for members of one's own sex. Both males and females may be homosexual; female homosexuals are usually referred to as ***lesbians***. It is difficult to determine the number of homosexuals in the United States. Sensitive questions in surveys about sexual behavior are subject to rather high levels of errors because respondents may not feel comfortable answering truthfully.

Early social scientists viewed homosexuality as a form of social pathology brought on by the disorganization of families and communities that were experiencing the effects of rapid urbanization and industrialization. Studies in the late 40s and 50s, however, began to make it clear that homosexuals were not distinguishable from heterosexuals psychologically and in other ways. Many of the deviant behaviors were reactions to social pressures rather than anything innate to homosexuality.

There is no convincing evidence that homosexuality is biologically determined. Some people believe there are genetic components in sexuality, but that does not necessarily mean a direct link. Some believe that homosexuality is learned and a matter of personal choice, which means that it can change.

Sociologists, psychiatrists, and anthropologists argue that the social environment plays a more important role than biological factors. They have observed that homosexuals tend to grow up in homes with a dominating, seductive mother, but they can't explain why all children from this kind of environment don't become homosexual.

Because lesbians are less conspicuous and because norms for women allow women to be closer, lesbianism is even more difficult to measure than male homosexuality. Also, because women mature differently, sexual experiences usually begin later for women and the first actual sexual experience for a lesbian is likely to come late during an intense emotional involvement.

The gay subculture refers to the visible institutions of the gay community. Undetermined proportions of homosexuals remain in the closet and do not participate openly in the gay community. However, in many large cities there are gay communities that allow homosexuals to live, work, shop, and be entertained in a largely gay milieu. A major function of the homosexual subculture is to give its members a way to understand and accept their sexual orientation.

Sexism and Gender Inequality

Sexism is the entire range of attitudes, beliefs, policies, laws, and behaviors discriminating against women (or against men) on the basis of their gender. Male dominance has persisted throughout the institutions of modern societies. Although political power and coercion play an important role in this dominance, ideology is also a key factor.

One of the unfortunate aspects of ideologies that support male dominance is that even people who are victimized by them tend to believe that they are true. That is, women can set up psychological barriers to their own achievement because they perceive success as being masculine or conform to conceptions of beauty that please males.

In employment, gender stereotyping has impacted the careers women (and men) choose and it has also impacted what they are paid. Women are more likely to be concentrated in lower-status jobs at the lower end of the pay scale, despite the fact that educational attainment for men and women is equal. Part of the explanation stems from differences in the number of years worked, as there are more interruptions in the work histories of women. While the number of women in traditionally male-dominated occupations has increased, they are still paid less than their male counterparts.

The difference between wages paid to male and female occupations is often referred to as the gender pay gap. **Table 8-3** indicates some of these patterns. The idea that pay levels of certain jobs should be adjusted to reflect the intrinsic value of the job is known as "comparable worth." While there has been an increase in the number of women in formerly male occupations, women are still paid less in those occupations. Wage and job discrimination is illegal, but continues to exist. There are numerous suits pending and some large settlements are reminding employers of the illegality.

Sexual harassment has received increased attention since the controversy around Clarence Thomas's nomination to the Supreme Court. The controversy has focused attention on serious forms of harassment, such as date rape, as well as behaviors that are annoying if not dangerous. People are moving toward consensus on norms of conduct between men and women and are increasingly recognizing behaviors that constitute sexual harassment.

Thousands of formal complaints are now being filed, but this still represents only a small fraction of the actual incidence of sexual harassment. Even rape is underreported. Sexual harassment is also extremely common in schools and other educational institutions. Both boys and girls experience it, and parents tend to accept it as a part of adolescence.

Sexual harassment includes continual or repeated verbal abuse of a sexual nature, including but not limited to graphic commentaries on the victim's body, sexually suggestive objects or postures in the workplace, sexually degrading words used to describe the victim, or propositions of a sexual nature. Sexual harassment also includes the threat or insinuation that lack of sexual submission will adversely affect the victim's employment, wages, standing, or other conditions that affect the victim's livelihood.

Women tend to bear primary responsibility for child care and housework, even if they work. Men who support nontraditional roles for women, do more. In Asia, Africa, and many parts of Latin America, homemaking remains the predominant concern of women.

Sources of Sexism

Sex role socialization is immensely important in forming our attitudes and behaviors as men and women. ***Socialization*** is a process whereby we learn to behave according to the norms of our culture. Most socialization takes place in interaction with other people, but also through popular culture. Research has shown that even as toddlers, boys and girls are treated differently and have different sets of expectations made of them.

Education represents a more formal type of socialization. Studies have shown that schools reinforce traditional sex role stereotypes and socialize children into traditional sex roles. Despite recent attempts to reduce the bias, women continue to achieve less well in math and science, and far fewer women are recruited into engineering and science. There is also some bias in career counseling, where girls are encouraged to pursue traditionally female-dominated professions.

Women homemakers often have a subordinate status within the home, which may limit their freedom and leave them feeling unfulfilled. Some researchers argue that more feminist researchers distort the extent to which women are dissatisfied with their homemaking roles. However, increasingly women are forced to both work and be a homemaker. Even if both husband and wife are professionals, the husband tends to have a more privileged position. It is assumed that the husband's career is more important and more effort is put into it. As a result, women are more likely to feel dissatisfied with their careers.

Language often reinforces stereotypes by over relying on male dominance terms and using stereotypical phrases in describing men and women. Sexism is most blatant in advertising. Advertising capitalizes on women's anxieties about perception. Women in the media are less likely to be portrayed as employed, few are shown in executive positions, and making fewer decisions.

Women participate in organized religion more than men, yet it is dominated by men both theologically and organizationally. Most churches bar women from performing the most sacred rituals or attaining the highest administrative posts. In recent decades there have been some changes, especially in more liberal denominations. Catholic women still face resistance from traditionalists in the Catholic hierarchy.

Although discrimination against women has received less overt support from government in recent years, patterns of discrimination still exist at all levels of government. In state and local government, women are underrepresented in high-level jobs and concentrated in lower-level, non-executive positions.

There are many legal barriers to sexual equality. Some state laws designed to protect workers discriminate against women. Sexual harassment complaints may take years to work through the legal system before a woman can win a chance at redress. Credit laws have changed, which make it easier for women to get home loans, but also make credit cards more accessible for low-income, single parent families. On a global scale, lack of credit has made it difficult for women to buy homes or start their own businesses.

Sources of Homophobia

Homophobia, or hostility towards homosexual individuals in general and gay men in particular, is a common aspect of the male gender identity in the United States and elsewhere. In recent years there has been a decrease in homophobia, although there are still a significant number of extremely hostile homophobic people.

The positive trend in public opinion regarding homosexuality is a result of years of political organizing. Gay activists continue to confront homophobia and develop campaigns to assert the legitimacy of gay and lesbian lifestyles.

Social Policy

The women's movement in the United States was officially founded in 1848, but declined after women received the right to vote in the 1920s. In the 1960s there was a resurgence of the movement. In 1964 Congress passed the Civil Rights Act, which included a provision (Title VII) that made it illegal to discriminate against women in promotion and hiring. The National Organization for Women (NOW) was established to pressure enforcement of Title VII.

Attitudes have begun to change and there has been a decrease in the double standard. Women's political participation has increased steadily. In the coming years the women's movement is likely to focus on single-parent families and, within this group, the special needs of low-income, female-headed families. On a global scale, women have learned to use the United Nations' information and communication systems effectively and have improved the health and economic well-being of women.

An important factor in full sexual equality is for fathers to share equally in the process and child rearing and homemaking. Family leave and increased benefits for part-time work could facilitate this. Child care is a significant issue for workfare mothers. They are using low-quality child care and are unaware of the childcare subsidies. These mothers are more depressed and their children are often noticeably retarded in many aspects of their development.

To eliminate sexism in education, teachers and school administrators must become more sensitive to their own stereotypes about boys and girls and treat both sexes equally. One way to counteract the idea that only women take care of children is to attract more male teachers to the lower grades. Repeal of affirmative action laws could impact equality in education. It is too soon to tell.

There are still gender differences in sentencing and the selection of juries. There are still complicated rules for filing discrimination cases and there are huge backlogs. Despite this, there have been some successful cases against discrimination. One area in which some progress has been made is known as comparable worth. The concept holds that the intrinsic value of different jobs can be measured and that jobs found to be of comparable value should receive comparable pay. Critics argue that there is no such thing as the intrinsic value of jobs.

Abortion is probably the single most controversial social and political issue in the United States. Antiabortion laws were passed in the mid-nineteenth century. Women continued to have abortions, and by the 1950s, agitation against existing laws caused a few states to permit abortion under certain circumstances. In 1970, New York State allowed abortion almost on demand; other states soon followed. In the 1990s the antiabortion movement suffered some setbacks because of the Clinton administration's strong support for pro-choice policies. In 2007, the Supreme Court ruled that certain forms of late-term abortion could be declared illegal, regardless of the danger to the woman's health if the pregnancy were continued.

Related to reproductive control is the availability of sex education and contraception. The need for abortion decreases as sex education and availability of contraceptives increases. Many poor women have less access to sex education and contraception.

The issues of women's rights have often eclipsed the need for men to examine and change their own sex roles. Inspired by the success of women, however, many men are exploring the roles that also limited them in the past. The opening up of fields that have traditionally been male or female to members of both sexes is likely to remain an important goal of the women's movement and civil rights organizations.

The issue of same-sex marriage, gays in the military, and custody of children in same-sex households remain extremely controversial. Legal recognition has been slow, but some large corporations are beginning to extend benefits to members of same-sex unions. Laws that try to control homosexual behavior have come under attack as violations of constitutional rights and attempts to legislate private morality.

The AIDS epidemic has raised the stakes in dealing with homosexual issues because it has revealed the need for open discussion for sexual practices among homosexuals. Although public service announcements about safe sex and condom use are more visible and widespread each year, the United States continues to lag far behind other affluent and highly literate societies in its acceptance of sex education and explicit discussions of AIDS and related problems. For safe sex campaigns to be effective, they must reach further than the gay community. However, this tends to elicit angry reactions.

Going Beyond Left and Right

It would be difficult to imagine an area of life in which there is more ideological and moral conflict in the United States than sexuality and gender. Issues like abortion often divide a group into conservatives and liberals. A society with diverse and strong opinions must try to reach compromises to achieve peace. There are no easy ways to resolve conflicts over sexual norms. A sociological approach to any issue emphasizes the need to look to the contexts of the different communities involved.

RESEARCH NAVIGATOR EXERCISES

ContentSelect

Select the sociology database. Use *gender inequality* as the keyword. The text discusses comparable worth and the ongoing disparity between men's and women's income. Read the article "Is There a Glass Ceiling Over Europe: Exploring the Gender Pay Gap Across the Wage Distribution" (*AN 23145067* – 1/07). What are the conclusions of this investigation? What are the major similarities between the United States and Europe when it comes to wage disparity?

New York Times Online

Use sociology as the subject, and enter the keyword *sex discrimination lawsuits*. Look for the 9/25/07 article, "Suit Claims Restaurant Looked Past Harassment," which deals with a federal Equal Employment Opportunity Commission lawsuit against Tavern on the Green (located in Central Park, NYC), accusing the restaurant of engaging in "severe and pervasive" harassment of employees, including a manager "grabbing female employee's" buttocks. Do you think enough is being done to combat sexual harassment? Why or why not?

Link Library

Use sociology as the subject, and click on G for Gender. Then click on gender issues. On the gender issues page, click on Gender in Picture Books. Read the article by Kay E. Vandergrift. What are Vandergrift's principal observations and conclusions? Do you agree or disagree with her assessment. What can you remember about the books you read in elementary and secondary school with regard to the portrayal of gender?

PRACTICE QUESTIONS

MULTIPLE CHOICE QUESTIONS: Select the one best answer for each of the following questions.

1. In 2004, the median income earned by full-time working women was ____ percent of men's income.
   a. 65 c. 87
   b. 52 d. 76

2. The majority of women in the United States
   a. don't work.
   b. continue to work in the "girl's ghetto" occupations.
   c. work in the professions.
   d. none of the above

3. Betty Friedan was one of the first contemporary feminists to identify and criticize the traditional view of female roles, which she labeled the
   a. pick-collar ghetto.
   b. second shift.
   c. feminine mystique.
   d. male hegenomy

4. The Equal Rights Amendment:
   a. passed in 1982.
   b. passed in 1983.
   c. has never been passed.
   d. is not promoted by women's rights activists.

5. ________ refers to a one's sense of one's attractiveness to others and a sense of comfort with one's body and one's feelings of sexual arousal.
   a. Gender identity
   b. Sexual identity
   c. Gender norms
   d. Sexual norms

6. ______ refers to a sense of maleness or femaleness.
   a. Sexual identity
   b. Gender identity
   c. Sexuality
   d. Sexual orientation

7. How one behaves sexually is termed _______.
   a. sexuality
   b. sexual orientation
   c. gender identity
   d. sexual identity

8. Which of the following is an accurate statement?
   a. Evelyn Hooker's research in the 1950s showed that homosexuals and heterosexuals are clearly distinguishable on any standardized projective tests.
   b. The American Psychiatric Association lists homosexuality as a form of mental illness.
   c. Most current research has produced convincing evidence that homosexuality is biologically determined.
   d. Social scientists argue that the social environment in which a person grows up plays as great a role in producing homosexuality as any biological factor.

9. Research conducted by R.W. Connell reveals that in much of the industrialized world
   a. men still have much greater access to cultural prestige, political authority, corporate power, individual wealth, and material comforts than women.
   b. individual men or small groups may be confused or insecure about the inequalities between men and women.
   c. with some notable exceptions, male-female relations are structured so that women are subordinate.
   d. all of the above

10. Wage discrimination is illegal under the
   a. Equal Pay Act of 1963.
   b. Comparable Work Act of 1986.
   c. Title XIV.
   d. none of the above

11. Sexual harassment
   a. came under public scrutiny in the early 1900s.
   b. has become less of a complaint among women.
   c. is among the most persistent and difficult aspects of sexism.
   d. has nothing to do with the Hill-Thomas controversy.

12. The text refers to law school professor, scholar, and pioneering social scientist Catherine MacKinnon as
   a. a strident feminist.
   b. a radical activist.
   c. a male bashing expert.
   d. an anti-harassment warrior.

13. According to the text, socialization
  a. is the process whereby we learn to behave according to the norms of our culture.
  b. includes all formal and informal teaching.
  c. usually takes place in the course of interaction with other people.
  d. all of the above

14. While sexism in everyday language is subtle and unconscious, in advertising it is
  a. nonexistent.
  b. only slightly more observable.
  c. often blatant.
  d. none of the above.

15. In comparison with men, women
  a. pray more often.
  b. attend church less frequently.
  c. dominate organized religion.
  d. None of the above.

16. Hostility, violence, and discrimination directed at people because they are homosexual, or suspected to be homosexual, is known as
  a. gay bashing.
  c. hegemony.
  b. homophobia.
  c. projection.

17. The women's movement in the United States initially began in order to
  a. free the slaves.
  b. win the right to vote.
  c. gain access to men's occupations.
  d. gain equal pay.

18. A 1984 Supreme Court ruling in *Grove City College v. Bell* established
  a. equal funding of all sports in professional schools.
  b. affirmative action programs in professional schools.
  c. that nondiscrimination in education is applied only to programs receiving federal aid and not to entire institutions.
  d. none of the above.

19. The idea that the pay levels of certain jobs should be adjusted so that they reflect the intrinsic value of the job is known as
  a. net worth.
  b. pay equity.
  c. comparable worth.
  d. income equity.

20. From the perspective of social policy, the text identifies ____ as a fascinating unintended consequence of the women's movement and one that is difficult to resolve through further policies.
  a. the persistence of the double standard
  b. Betty Friedan's feminine mystique
  c. Arlie Hochschild's second shift
  d. none of the above

ESSAY QUESTIONS

1. Are traditional sex roles positive or negative? Explain.

2. Describe and discuss some of the attitudes and practices that are part of sexism in our society.

3. List and describe the various sources of sexism.

4. Discuss the various changes necessary for the elimination of sexism.

5. How might the policy of "comparable worth" be implemented?

ANSWERS TO MULTIPLE CHOICE QUESTIONS

1.	d	11.	c
2.	b	12.	d
3.	c	13.	d
4.	c	14.	c
5.	a	15.	a
6.	b	16.	b
7.	a	17.	a
8.	d	18.	c
9.	d	19.	c
10.	a	20.	c

CHAPTER NINE

An Aging Society

CHAPTER OUTLINE

I. Aging as a Social Problem
    A. Perspectives on Aging
II. The Elderly in America Today
    A. Age Stratification
    B. Who Are the Elderly?
        1. The Uneven Graying of America
    C. Ageism
III. Dimensions of the Aging Process
    A. Physiological Aspects of Aging
        1. Chronological Aging
        2. Primary and Secondary Aging
    B. Psychological Dimensions of Aging
    C. Social and Cultural Dimensions of Aging
        1. The Aged as a Minority Group
        2. Myths and Stereotypes about the Elderly
IV. Concomitants of Aging
    A. Victimization of the Elderly
    B. Elder Abuse
    C. Health Care and the Aged
    D. Economic Discrimination
        1. Multiple Jeopardy
    E. Family Problems
        1. Grandparents Raising Grandchildren
V. Retirement
VI. Death
        1. Death with Dignity
VII. Social Policy
    A. Housing
    B. Health Care
    C. Retirement and Social Security
    D. Future Prospects
VIII. Going Beyond Left and Right
IX. Summary
X. Key Terms
XI. Social Problems Online
XII. Research Navigator

LEARNING OBJECTIVES

After reading Chapter Nine you should:

1. Be able to distinguish how functionalists, interactionists, and conflict theorists would approach aging.
2. Know how to define age stratification and discuss what impact it could have on the elderly.
3. Understand the changes in the proportion of elderly in American society and know how social scientists define specific groups within the elderly population.
4. Be able to define ageism and discuss its impact on the elderly.
5. Know the differences among chronological aging, primary aging, and secondary aging.
6. Know how the aged are like a minority group and why they are called a "quasi-minority" group.
7. Understand some of the myths and stereotypes about the elderly and why they are inaccurate.
8. Be able to discuss some of the concomitants of aging and the effects they have on the elderly.
9. Understand the economic impact of retirement from the point of view of the whole society.
10. Know why understanding the process of death is important.

KEY TERMS

ageism
modernization
age stratification
gerontology
primary aging
secondary aging
hospices

CHAPTER SUMARY

Aging as a Social Problem

A major source of structural strain in societies is the long-term failure of social institutions to accommodate the increasing proportion of the population that is elderly. The social problems associated with certain age groups, especially the very young and the very old, are aggravated by three factions, which all have an impact on the roles assigned to people of different ages: labeling, the concept of work as the basis of personal value, and economic deprivation.

In the past several decades, the economic status of the aged as a group has improved markedly; the average income of older people is about 90 percent of that of younger adults. The elderly are not a homogeneous group, however; and there are still large numbers of older people who experience economic insecurity because of their vulnerability to major costs, such as medical expenses that are not fully covered by insurance.

Aging as a social problem is often studied from the point of view of one or more of the basic perspective described in Chapter 1. The functionalist perspective views aging as a problem because the institutions in modern society are not working well enough to serve the needs of the dependent aged. The elderly are rendered useless as their functions are replaced by those of other social institutions.

Interactionists see the term elderly as a stigmatizing label; it suggests that older people are less valuable because they do not conform to the norms of a youth-oriented culture. Interactionists view the elderly as victims of ***ageism***, or forms of prejudice and discrimination that are directed at them not only by individuals but also by social institutions.

Conflict theorists believe that the problems of the elderly stem from their lack of power to shape social institutions to meet the needs of people who are no longer in their productive years and have not accumulated the means to preserve their economic and social independence. Conflict theorists argue that the aged must band together to assert their need for meaningful lives and adequate social services. **Table 9-2** summarizes these perspectives' views on aging as a social problem.

The Elderly in America Today

In the United States and most Western countries, the productive and cultural roles of the aged have been weakened by industrialization and the migration of family members to cities. In this sense, the problems of the aged are part of the larger complex of social changes known as ***modernization***, which is the transformation of societies to urbanized and industrialized ways of life based on scientific technologies, individualized rather than communal or collective roles, and a cosmopolitan outlook that values efficiency and progress.

Modernization and progress are not equivalent. Modernizations brings new social problems and, sometimes, new solutions. Modernization is associated with increasing length of live, but this is positive only when quality of life is enhanced. Technology and science has increased life spans, which, as a result, have increased the number of elderly people. Modern societies all over the globe have begun to deal with poverty and illness among their elderly citizens. As more people live longer, the proportion with major medical problems increases, as does the need for costly medical care. This means that society as a whole needs to improve the quality of life for the most elderly among the population and to find ways to care for a growing number of frail and ill elderly people.

Urbanization is also associated with modernization. Younger people have migrated to Sunbelt cities to find employment, leaving elderly in rural areas or industrial cities of the North and Midwest. The result is a higher concentration of elderly in these areas.

Riley and Waring have described the process of ***age stratification***. Age operates like race or class in segregating people into different groups or strata. Like class, age can limit access to certain roles and access to good things in life. Old people may react by becoming dependent or disengaged or by manifesting the kinds of behavior that are labeled as senile.

Age stratification may also lead to age segregation and conflict. In the wake of age segregation come suspicion, mistrust, and hostility. The young lack confidence in their elderly; the old often fear the young. Isolation of age groups and intergenerational conflicts are common.

Recently, social scientists have begun to identify specific groups within the growing population of the elderly, such as the "young-old" (65-75 years) or the "frail old," who cannot carry out the basic activities of life without help.

Demographers in the U.S. Census Bureau estimate that in the twenty-first century the elderly will be the fastest growing segment of the population as the huge Baby Boom generation enters its later years. By 2050 more than one-fifth of the U.S. population is expected to be over the age of 65.

The elderly are not evenly distributed over the continent. Two-thirds of the elderly live in urban areas, many in central cities; they also represent the highest proportion of the population in small towns. As a result of migration, many retired people live in the West and South.

One attitude that contributes to ageism is the inordinate value placed on youthful looks, especially for women. Another source of ageism is the belief that the old are useless; since they do not work and cannot reproduce, they are perceived to serve no purpose. Ageism as a social problem is also confounded with sexism. Feminist social scientists ask whether ageism would be a problem if men outlived women instead of the reverse. Ageism prevails in government, where funding of the aged is frequently cut first. Ageism is reflected in the practice of mandatory retirement.

The mass media play a part in promoting ageism. Television, for example, persists in portraying the elderly as weak in both body and mind, and as a burden on their relatives. There is evidence that the aging of the American population may be resulting in some value shifts. Respect for age has been highly rated in recent opinion polls. The difficulties of the old are mirrored by their higher-than-average suicide rate, particularly for older males. Older men are almost five times more likely to commit suicide than older women. This may in part be due to the loss of social attachments.

Dimensions of the Aging Process

One dimension of the aging process involves physiological aspects. Chronological aging, the simple accumulation of years, is a largely automatic process. Not everyone ages at the same rate, however. ***Gerontology***, the study of the process and causes of aging, attempts to identify the physical causes and effects of the aging process and to control the factors that diminish the rewards of a long life.

There are two categories in the aging process: **primary aging**, the result of molecular and cellular changes, and **secondary aging**, an accelerated version of normal aging that is caused by environmental factors: lack of exercise, stress, trauma, poor diet, and disease. The effects of primary aging are seen in wrinkles, gray hair, and increased susceptibility to disease. As the body ages, its systems degenerate.

Aging is a gradual process; not all the body's systems age at the same rate. Some researchers are convinced that each of us carries a personal timetable for aging with our cells, a timetable that is controlled by our genes. Others believe that secondary aging factors are also involved.

There is evidence that many of the effects of aging are neither inevitable nor irreversible. For example, reduced oxygen intake, diminished lung capacity, and slow circulation and related mental and physical problems are results not just of age but also of the inactivity that may come with it.

The aging process also produces psychological effects as well as physical ones. Social factors also influence the psychological consequences of aging. New roles always require some adjustment, but for the elderly this adjustment is complicated because their new roles are poorly defined; there are few role models or reference groups on which they can pattern their behavior. This makes them more dependent on labels and opinions of others for their self-determination. These labels are usually negative, which causes psychological difficulties.

False assumptions about the inevitability of senility account for much of the misunderstanding we have about the psychological effects of aging. Contrary to what many people believe, the human brain does not necessarily deteriorate with age. Negative attitudes about the elderly cause many people to consider an older person senile when in fact that person is merely depressed. Depression can cause such symptoms as confusion and loss of certain intellectual abilities.

Social gerontologists frequently refer to the aged as a minority group, pointing out that the elderly exhibit many characteristics of such groups and, like minority groups, are victims of prejudice, stereotyping, and discrimination. Unlike traditional minority groups, however, the elderly do not exist as an independent subgroup; everyone has the potential to grow old. Sometimes they are called a "quasi-minority" group.

The potential power of this quasi-minority group is enormous. There are more of them, but they themselves are changing. They are becoming more active in politics and in other voluntary organizations.

Popular culture characterizes old people as senile, lacking in individuality, tranquil, nonproductive, conservative, and resistant to change. There is abundant evidence to the contrary. Some of the most pernicious myths about the elderly are directed against older women. Research shows that these myths simply are not true. These myths relate to such things as health, marriage, widowhood, and the "rocking-chair image."

One of the most widely accepted stereotypes about the old is that they are sexually inactive because of both lack of desire and lack of ability. Research has shown that although sexual interest and activity tend to decline with age, sex continues to play an important role in the lives of older people.

Concomitants of Aging

The elderly do not view themselves as likely victims of crime, even though the media do. Because many elderly live in high-crime areas, they run a risk of being victimized. Elderly people are frequent victims of a wide variety of business crimes that prey on their desire for security and comfort. Law enforcement authorities cannot accurately state the amount of loss caused by such swindles, but it is estimated to total hundreds of millions of dollars annually.

In the United States and other aging societies, there is growing awareness of mental and physical abuse of elderly people. In recent testimony before Congress, it was estimated that there are at least 1.5 million cases of physical abuse of elderly people in the United States each year, and many experts view this as a conservative estimate because it does not include mental cruelty or severe neglect. While most of the abuse occurs in private households, a significant proportion of reported cases occur in nursing homes and other institutional settings.

Because people are living longer, the elderly are more prone to chronic illnesses, which develop over a long period and are often expensive to treat. Thus, the elderly tend to require increasing amounts of costly medical care, which they are unable to afford. As the number of elderly people continues to increase, the problems of funding adequate health coverage for the elderly, for whom long-term care is often a necessary and costly requirement, remain a major issue. Medicare and Medicaid help, but they do not cover all health-care expenses.

There are about 1.5 million people in nursing homes, often not because they require constant attention but because no alternative services are available. Unnecessary institutionalization of the elderly is costly in terms of both public spending and the negative psychological effects on occupants.

Older Americans are frequently the targets of job discrimination; the most common form is mandatory retirement. Older workers also encounter job discrimination when seeking new employment. The Social Security system has been modified so that the retirement age will increase in the next few years. However, the purpose is to reduce financial pressure on the program, not to reduce economic discrimination against the elderly.

To be old, black (or Hispanic or Native American), and female is to experience multiple jeopardy, facing more hardships than one would face if one were in just one or two of these categories. Elderly blacks are more likely to be poor and to suffer poor health. Women of all races face disadvantages in old age. There are more than 20 million elderly women in American, and many of them have financial problems.

One of the most pervasive myths about the aged is that their children abandon them. Most old people who live alone do so voluntarily. The institutionalized elderly are not typical. Most suffer physical or mental disorders and have outlived their families. As people live longer, more elderly people have elderly parents they must care for while facing the problems of aging themselves. Changes in the roles of women are also complicating things. Women are more likely to work outside the home, but are still expected to be caregivers for elderly parents and in-laws.

A growing number of elderly people in the United States are facing the unexpected task of raising grandchildren. Sociologists refer to this pattern as the "skipped-generation" household.

From the point of view of society, retirement creates problems because those who are no longer in the labor force are dependent on the wealth produced by those who are still working. This problem of increasing dependency ratios poses a threat to the Social Security and Medicare systems. Extending the average working years could help. This is more popular than one might imagine, as significant numbers of workers would prefer to work as long as possible.

Death and old age have always been closely linked, but today more people live to old age and the association is stronger. Social scientists study death in terms of its psychological and social impact. Their research indicates that the old, perhaps because of a natural process of disengagement, have less fear of death than the young. Research suggests that there is a distinct pattern of feelings and behaviors that emerges during the process of death, known as the dying trajectory, which differs from one person to another and from one situation to another.

By understanding the dying process, physicians, caretakers, friends, and family members can make the experience easier for the dying person. ***Hospices***, special institutions designed for the terminally ill, are as comfortable and homelike as possible and are staffed by personnel who are trained in working with the dying. Because of life-prolonging technology, people are faced with choices about how to die. "Death with dignity" has become a popular phrase as people confront the issues of relegating the old and the terminally ill to institutions and to a life sustained by machines. Surveys indicate that people would prefer to die at home. Medicare now supports home hospice care.

Social Policy

The primary social policy issues concerning the elderly are housing, health care, and retirement and Social Security. Most elderly people who live with their children or other younger relatives do so for financial reasons or because of declining health. Most would prefer to continue living where they are.

It is the very old who are in nursing homes, and they tend to suffer from dementia or physical infirmities, which will require an increase in public funds from $18 billion as this population increases. Currently, there is little legislation that is designed to help with housing programs for disabled elderly people.

Because of the rapid growth in the elderly population, Medicare, the federal program that provides health care for the elderly, is in financial trouble. The problem is that payments to doctors and hospitals are rising faster than payroll taxes that fund Medicare. Some elderly are distributing their wealth to living relatives through living trusts that enable them to protect their savings from the costs of long-term care. As the 2008 presidential election approaches, the nation's elderly voters are being heavily courted by all the potential candidates.

Prescription drug coverage for the elderly is increasingly becoming a political issue. Republicans are attempting to increase coverage by subsidizing private insurance companies. Democrats would prefer a larger role for the government in providing the coverage.

The Social Security system was not designed to be the main source of income for the elderly. It was originally intended as a form of insurance against unexpected reductions in income due to retirement, disability, or the death of a wage-earning spouse. For many people, this is the source of retirement income, and the system is not financed to support this. Other problems are that it discriminates against women and it denies that the elderly can and should remain productive. The author discusses the president's "ownership approach" to Social Security reform.

As the Baby Boom generation continues to age, government and the media will pay more attention to the problems of aging.

Going Beyond Left and Right

What right do people have to take their own lives? What right do governments have to intervene in such a private decision? The behavior of the elderly (living wills and "do not resuscitate" orders) seems to suggest that many take the position that these matters are best resolved by individuals, their doctors, and their families.

RESEARCH NAVIGATOR

ContentSelect

Select the sociology database and enter the keywords *the elderly and Social Security*. Look for research on Social Security and social welfare programs for the elderly. Read the article entitled "Comparing the Impacts of Social Security Benefit Reduction on the Income Distribution of the Elderly" (*AN 21890124*) (6/07). How do the findings of this article fit into the text's discussion of income distribution among the aging population of the United States?

New York Times Online
Use sociology as the subject, then, use the keyword *retirement*. Look for the article by Stuart Elliott (10/4/2007), entitled "Tailoring Messages to a New Audience: Wrinkled Baby Boomers." In this article, Elliott discusses how the deluge of Baby Boomers into older age opens up a new category for marketing and advertising in the United States. Beginning in 2008, over 10,000 Baby Boomers per day will apply for Social Security. How do you think the Baby Boom generation will affect the nation over the next several decades?

Link Library
Use sociology as the subject, then click on A for aging. From the list of public sites, select Social Gerontology and the Aging Revolution. Scroll down this page until you find Outline of Page. Below this, look for social psychology of aging and the double and triple jeopardy hypotheses. What does double and triple jeopardy mean in this context? Ask a parent or grandparent or an older acquaintance how they feel about this. How will you feel when you reach this age? Next, look at the politics of aging. Be sure to examine the information on Social Security. This is a program that affects young and old alike, as it is a regressive tax (it borrows from the young to care for the old). What are some of the strengths and weaknesses of this program? If Social Security is privatized, how will those who are poor fare? Is it reasonable to assume that a poor worker will be able to set aside funds for retirement? What risks, if any, do you see for the poor?

PRACTICE QUESTIONS

MULTIPLE CHOICE QUESTIONS: Select the one best answer for each of the following questions.

1. Which of the following regions of the world has the highest percentage of aged as part of their respective populations?
   a. Oceania
   b. North America
   c. Europe
   d. Asia

2. In approaching the problems affecting the elderly, interactionists
   a. see the term elderly as a label that stigmatizes the aged in American society.
   b. emphasize that older people are less valuable because they do not conform to the norms of a youth-oriented culture.
   c. view the elderly as valued role models for the young.
   d. argue that the elderly should band together to realize their potential political power.

3. ______ refers to the transformation of societies to urbanized and industrialized ways of life based on scientific technologies, individualized rather than communal or collective roles, and a cosmopolitan outlook that values efficiency and progress.
   a. Postindustrialism
   b. Modernization
   c. Progress
   d. Democratization

4. According to the text's discussion, age stratification
   a. limits the kinds of roles that the members of different age groups can hold.
   b. seems, to some degree, to be acceptable and even inevitable.
   c. may produce some of the disengagement that is common among elderly people.
   d. all of the above

5. According to the text, the category labeled the "oldest-old" refers to people
   a. between the ages of 65 and 75.
   b. over the age of 75.
   c. over the age of 85.
   d. over the age of 65, but who are in poor health.

6. Many attitudes that are prevalent in modern society contribute to the devaluation of the aged, a phenomenon that is referred to as
   a. ageism.
   b. elder bashing.
   c. elder abuse.
   d. age stereotyping.

7. Collectively, the characteristics that we associate with advancing years, such as gray hair, wrinkles, and increased susceptibility to disease, are known as _____ aging.
   a. chronological
   b. primary
   c. secondary
   d. stereotypical

8. According to the text's discussion of the psychological dimension of aging,
   a. the new roles of the elderly are poorly defined.
   b. the elderly have few role models or reference groups on which they can pattern their behavior.
   c. older people become dependent on labels and on the opinions of others for their self-definition.
   d. all of the above

9. Senility in the aged is
   a. common by age 70.
   b. frequently depression.
   c. never associated with age.
   d. more common among women than men.

10. Which of the following is NOT one of the myths about the elderly?
   a. The elderly are viewed by social gerontologists as a minority group.
   b. Older women tend to be hypochondriacs.
   c. Widows usually based their identities on their deceased husbands.
   d. Older women typically confine their interests to knitting and rocking by the fireside.

11. One of the reasons the elderly may be at risk of victimization is
   a. senility.
   b. impaired vision.
   c. they are more likely to live in high-crime areas.
   d. they can't run as fast.

12. The problem with elderly abuse
   a. has decreased in the past 10 years.
   b. is a myth.
   c. affects over 1.5 million elders annually.
   d. receives adequate attention in the media and from the government.

13. Research on the elderly indicates that among the black population
    a. poverty is three times white poverty rates.
    b. overall health is superior to whites.
    c. Social Security is more available and utilized.
    d. economic conditions are improving.

14. Which of the following is true about elderly women?
    a. They are less likely to go to the doctor than elderly men.
    b. They are not interested in sex.
    c. If widowed, they maintain no self-identity.
    d. They are increasingly devalued by society.

15. The best-known description of the dying trajectory was proposed in the classic work of
    a. Emile Durkheim.
    b. Elisabeth Kübler-Ross.
    c. Thomas Szasz.
    d. Robert Merton.

16. Death is increasingly associated with old age because
    a. young people stereotype the elderly.
    b. more people are reaching old age.
    c. the dying process is better understood.
    d. hospice programs are more effective.

17. Research indicates that during the process of dying a distinct pattern of feelings and behavior emerges. This pattern is referred to as the dying ____.
    a. response cycle
    b. trajectory
    c. identity shift
    d. curve

18. Among the aged between the ages of 65-74, what percentage live in nursing homes?
    a. 2
    b. 6
    c. 8
    d. 10

19. Annual prescription drug costs for senior citizens covered by Medicare average about $____.
    a. 860
    b. 1100
    c. 2600
    d. 3200

20. Perhaps the greatest flaw in the Social Security system is that
    a. its benefits are too small for the purpose they must serve.
    b. the system will bankrupt itself in two or three decades.
    c. people view it as a stand-alone retirement program.
    d. the government is incompetent to manage it.

ESSAY QUESTIONS

1. Discuss the economic impact of a higher ratio of elderly to young people from the perspective of society as a whole.

2. Describe the impact of aging on health care and health-care coverage.

3. Discuss how functionalists, interactionists, and conflict theorists view the problems associated with aging.

4. Define primary and secondary aging.

5. Discuss why social scientists talk about the elderly as a quasi-minority group rather than a minority group. Identify the similarities and differences between the two concepts.

6. Explain "multiple jeopardy." Which groups within the elderly population does it refer to?

7. Discuss Kübler-Ross's stages of the dying process.

ANSWERS TO MULTIPLE CHOICE QUESTIONS

1.	a	11.	c
2.	b	12.	c
3.	b	13.	a
4.	d	14.	d
5.	c	15.	b
6.	a	16.	b
7.	a	17.	b
8.	d	18.	a
9.	b	19.	d
10.	a	20.	a

CHAPTER TEN

The Changing Family

CHAPTER OUTLINE

I. The Nature of Families
   A. Adequate Family Functioning
   B. Effects of Women's Employment
      1. Juggling Work and Family Responsibilities
   C. The Black Family
II. Divorce
   A. The New "Divorce Divide"
   B. Explanations of Trends in Divorce Rates
   C. The Impact of Divorce
   D. Stepfamilies
   E. Cohabiting Couples
III. Postponement of Marriage
IV. Changing Norms of Parenthood
   A. Births to Unmarried Women
   B. Teenage Pregnancy
   C. Gay and Lesbian Families
V. Homeless Families
      1. Shelter Poverty and Homelessness
VI. Family Violence
   A. Child Abuse
   B. Spouse Abuse
VII. Social Policy
   A. Divorce Law
      1. The Ongoing Debate over Divorce Law
      2. Alimony
      3. Child Support
   B. Efforts to Reduce Teenage Pregnancies
      1. Abstinence Only, Abstinence Not
   C. Child Care and Family Support
   D. Future Prospects
VIII. Going Beyond Left and Right
IX. Summary
X. Key Terms
XI. Social Problems Online
XII. Research Navigator

LEARNING OBJECTIVES

After reading Chapter Ten you should:

1. Know the differences among nuclear, extended, and modified extended families.

2. Understand the impact women entering the workforce has had on the nuclear family.
3. Understand how black families may differ from white families and what some of the factors causing these differences might be.
4. Be familiar with how the rates of divorce have changed during the last century and how that has affected families.
5. Be able to describe how divorce affects families and the impact it has on women.
6. Know who are likely to cohabitate, and describe the stability and endurance of such relationships.
7. Be familiar with how the stigma of premarital pregnancy has changed and the legal implications of being an unwed mother.
8. Know how the rates of teenage pregnancy have changed and what factors led to those changes.
9. Know about the changing legal implications of same-sex marriages.
10. Be able to describe some of the social policies designed to bolster family values and their effectiveness.

KEY TERMS

kinship unit
nuclear family
extended family
modified extended family
shelter poverty
child abuse
alimony
abstinence only program

CHAPTER SUMMARY

The Nature of Families

A ***kinship unit*** is a group of individuals who are related to one another by blood, marriage, or adoption. Definitions of kinship differ from one society to another. In some societies the basic kinship group is the ***nuclear family***: a father, a mother, and their children, living apart from other kin. In other societies, a more common type of kinship group is the ***extended family:*** parents, children, grandparents, aunts, uncles, and others living together or in very close proximity. Increasingly, societies exhibit another type of kinship group, the ***modified extended family***, in which the individual nuclear families live separately but the extended family remains a strong kinship organization through a combination of interpersonal attachments and various forms of economic exchanges and mutual aid.

The nuclear family is the predominant kinship group in hunting and gathering societies and in industrial societies, whereas the extended family is more likely to be found in agrarian societies. However, changes in family form and function in the United States and other large contemporary societies suggest that many different family forms are possible and will coexist under different economic and social conditions.

Industrialization seems to promote the development of smaller family units that are more mobile, both geographically and socially. Functionalists say that industrialization, urbanization, and modern technology decrease the functions of the extended family and increase the functions of the nuclear family.

All families are continually undergoing change because they must constantly adapt to a family cycle of development in which the roles of all family members will change. Failure to function adequately could lead to problems within the family. Such failure is usually involuntary, resulting from either external or internal crises. External crises such as war and economic recession disrupt the family from the outside. Internal crises arise within the family, for example, when a family member suffers a serious physical or mental disorder.

These stresses and other interpersonal problems may reduce the family to an "empty shell," one that is held together not so much by feelings of warmth and attraction as by outside pressures. Less attention is devoted to marriages that remain vital throughout the partners' lives, and sociologists are only beginning to understand what makes marriages long lasting.

In the traditional concept of the American family, the husband worked in the paid labor force and the wife worked at home. Today, over 70 percent of American women with children under the age of 18 work outside the home. Much of the conflict over family issues and over the sharing of domestic and economic roles stems from this major change.

Most sociologists agree that the movement of women out of the home and into the labor force is one of the most important trends of the second half of the twentieth century. Despite this massive transformation, attitudes about working mothers have not changed as fast. Several studies have concluded that if the wife works outside the home as a matter of choice, the marriage is as happy as or happier than it would be if she chose to remain at home; if she works out of necessity, marital happiness suffers.

Most evidence does not support the traditional view that women are fulfilled by a domestic role. Arlie Hochschild found that women who work have less time for themselves and often think of the work they do in the home as a kind of "second shift." A follow-up study by Kathleen Gerson found that many men are beginning to shoulder more of the responsibility for domestic tasks. However, her study also found that a significant proportion of men were deciding that a single life was easier.

A common theme in all urban industrial societies is the difficulty of juggling work and family responsibilities, especially for women and especially as more hours are worked. Polls often reveal that women with young children would prefer to stay home, but economic conditions and the desire to achieve and maintain a middle-class lifestyle often oblige both parents to work.

In some cases the woman may have advanced further in her career than her husband and he may stay home to care for children. This imbalance in the traditional norm has created stresses in some marriages and innovative role changes in others.

One consequence of the difficulties couples encounter in juggling work and family roles is that marital happiness often decreases when children are born. As a result, growing numbers of couples are postponing childbirth or deciding not to have children at all.

In African-American communities, rates of marriage vary positively with education; better-educated women are far more likely to marry than are less educated women. Among whites, the relationship is reversed. Education is another important determinant of family stability. African Americans aged 18 to 24 who are not in school and have not finished high school decreased in the 1990s, but the proportion has begun to increase. Income and education are major factors in explain black-white differences in the marital status of men. Insofar as the black family is distinctive, it is probably a consequence of the special intensity and duration of the poverty and discrimination suffered by African Americans.

Divorce

All but unheard of in the nineteenth century and still rare before World War I, divorce and remarriage have become commonplace in American society. In recent years the divorce rate has risen among college-educated couples and those in higher socioeconomic groups. The highest rate of divorce, amounting to about one-third of all divorces, occurs in the first three years of marriage.

It is commonly believed that having children cements marriages, but research has shown that having babies early in a marriage does not make a couple happier and often makes them less happy. In general, couples who are not happy in their relationships often become less so when babies arrive. On a global scale, the phenomenon of divorce appears to be closely linked to modernization, regardless of the particular religion that is dominant in a nation.

Recent analysis of divorce rates in the United States and other industrialized nations indicates that there is a widening gap between divorce rates among people with high levels of education and those with less education. This pattern has been described as the "divorce divide."

One force that puts pressure on marriage is the change from extended to nuclear families. Another factor is the extent to which functions that were formerly performed by the family have been assumed by outside agencies. Other factors include the relaxation of attitudes about divorce, the reformation of divorce laws so that divorces are easier to obtain, and the growing number of educated women who can earn a living independently.

Divorce is almost always accompanied by considerable emotional and financial strain. This is especially true for women. Divorced mothers are frequently forced into poverty and dependence on public assistance. Children may experience divorce as the end of life as they knew it. They feel fear, anger, depression, and confusion. Research has shown that many divorced parents are unable to meet the challenges of parenting and instead depend on the children to help them cope. The result is an "overburdened child" who must not only handle normal stresses of childhood but also help a parent avoid depression. There are three common sources of strain after divorce: responsibility overload, task overload, and emotional overload. These factors, rather than the number of parents in the home, may be crucial to children's adjustment.

Nearly 50 percent of families in the United States are stepfamilies, and the number is growing continually. Recent studies indicate that stepmothers typically work quite hard to be good parents to their stepchildren. However, it is also true that combining children in a new family often adds conflict and tension to family life.

Cohabitation is most common among people under 25 and over 65. Recent data show that about half of all cohabitation relationships last less than a year, and that only 10 percent of cohabitation couples are still together after six years.

Postponement of Marriage

Postponement of marriage became more common in the decades following World War II as young people chose to concentrate on education and careers. One implication is that the average number of children per family has decreased. Another implication is that people are grandparents for shorter periods of time. It also means that the proportion of childless couples increases. Since men tend to marry women who are younger than themselves, the number of women who would like to marry is greater than the number of available men.

Changing Norms of Parenthood

In our society, many of the stigmas traditionally associated with premarital pregnancy have been reduced. However, many of the distinctive difficulties of unwed mothers (as opposed to widowed or divorced) are a matter of legal status. Single mothers do not often have the resources to pursue deadbeat dads. New efforts are being made to enforce compliance with court orders of child support for all children, regardless of the parent's marital status. Many sociologists view the weakening of marital norms as one of the greatest and most negative changes in the family as a major institution of modern society.

Teenage birth rates have fallen to the lowest level in four decades, but are still higher than other urban industrialized nations, who provide their teenagers with more sex education, more access to birth control, and superior health institutions.

A persistent issue in the United States is whether young women who become pregnant should be allowed to have abortions. The impact of abortion on young women's lives remains an area of controversy and continued research. One two-year study that followed teenagers who had an abortion and those who gave birth, found more positive results for those who had the abortion. However, critics argue that two years was not enough time to produce meaningful results.

Throughout the United States, the number of same-sex marriages is on the rise, although there is controversy about the legal status of such marriages. Major corporations like Disney and Xerox are extending health and other insurance to the domestic partners of gay and lesbian employees. In order to get these benefits, employees must declare their partnerships, which could create homophobic reactions in the workplace. The AIDS epidemic has led homosexual couples to consider longer-term relationships and, in doing so, the desire to have children.

Many gay and lesbian couples consider themselves to be married, and an estimated one-third of lesbians and one-fifth of gay males have children from previous heterosexual marriages. Changes in adoption and advances in artificial insemination have led to in increase in same-sex couples with children.

Homeless Families

Some estimates put the number of homeless families at about 750,000, depending on the time of year, the state of the economy, and the availability of low-cost housing. When families must pay more than 30 percent of their monthly income for rent or other housing parents, social scientists refer to them as "shelter poor."

Family Violence

Child abuse is a serious problem in the Untied States. ***Child abuse*** may be defined as a deliberate attack on a child by a parent or other caregiver that results in physical injury. A major obstacle to research on this topic is concern for the traditional rights of parents, who have the right to inflict physical violence on their children (e.g., spanking and other corporal punishment). Protection of the traditional rights of the family may prevent authorities from intervening or even knowing about child abuse. Some researchers estimate that only one case in three is ever discovered.

Characteristics of families in which abuse occurs include one or more of the following: 1) there is only one parent, 2) the parent's socioeconomic status and level of education are low, 3) the parent is highly authoritarian, 4) the family includes four or more children and has received some kind of public assistance within a year of abuse, and 5) the family changes its place of residence frequently. Research on child abuse is biased towards the poor, but some studies suggest that rather than the problems of poverty, abuse may be associated with personality patterns of abusive parents and their history of abuse.

Violence between spouses has long be acknowledged and even tolerated as part of domestic life. Wives are the most frequent victims, although cases of battered husbands have sometimes been reported. Like child abuse, it has been difficult to study spouse abuse, and authorities have been reluctant to intervene. Recently, laws have changed and police are better trained to deal with it.

A surprising number of women make no attempt to leave the men who abuse them. Researchers suggest that this results from dependence on the abusive man and "learned helplessness." There is a high correlation between child abuse and spouse abuse. A battered wife may remain with her husband in an attempt to protect the children. Conversely, the children may try to intervene and defend their mother, thereby causing the father to turn on them.

Social Policy

There is not much evidence to support the claim that social policies intended to bolster family values and morality make a great deal of difference. However, policies that improve the economic situations of families, allowing married couples to avoid the intense stress of poverty and unemployment, or debt and bankruptcy, do help.

Many states have liberalized their divorce laws and moved toward the concept of no-fault divorce. No-fault divorce laws allow judges to decide on such issues as child custody and division of property without blaming one partner or the other. Several states are considering measures that would make it more difficult for couples to divorce, especially if they have children. Some states are creating a voluntary "covenant" form of marriage in which couples sign a contract that requires them to seek counseling when they experience marital difficulties and forbids them to invoke no-fault reasons for divorce.

Alimony, or the money paid by one partner for the support of the other, usually by the husband to the wife, has been closely tied to the concept of fault in divorce proceeding. When a decree of divorce can be granted without the need to punish either partner, alimony can be awarded on the more realistic basis of financial need and ability to provide.

Children often suffer economically as a result of divorce. Policy makers have focused on the child-support system as a way to reduce high poverty rates among children in single-parent families. A high priority of family courts is to track down ex-husbands who fail to pay for the support of their children. The federal government and many states have instituted tougher policies on enforcement of child-support payments. In many states, child-support payments to women receiving TANF benefits go to the state to offset her family assistance. This could create disincentives for mothers to report nonpayment of child support.

The 1996 Welfare Reform Act attempt to reduce teenage pregnancy by cutting off aid to teenage mothers. The theory is that they have babies for the support. Most sociologists who study this issue believe that this reasoning is flawed.

Sex education and access to birth control have been shown to reduce rates of teenage pregnancy. At this writing, Congress is preparing to cut the funding for so-called ***abstinence-only programs***. Despite the substantial social-scientific evidence, it is unlikely that there will be federal support of increased access to birth control or sex education directed toward teenagers. It is likely that there will be new policy initiatives to make unmarried fathers more responsible for the support of their offspring.

Communities and government need to assist parents in caring for their children. Such assistance might include medical care, day care for the children of working parents, early childhood education, after-school learning programs, summer recreation, and so on. For more and more families child-care services in the community are becoming a necessity of family life. The Family Leave Act requires businesses to allow leaves, with or without pay, to mothers and fathers of newborn children.

Going Beyond Left and Right

Issues bearing on families and family responsibilities produce passionate debate. One major debate revolves around individual versus social responsibility. Liberals tend to focus on those in need, while conservatives tend to focus more on poor individual decisions that led to those needs. Sociological analysis tends to take a pragmatic approach on this issue. A major question here concerns what needs to be done. Sociologists attempt to provide facts, evaluations of existing approaches, and unimpassioned answers to ease the tensions aroused by angry debates over values.

RESEARCH NAVIGATOR EXERCISES

ContentSelect

Use the sociology database and enter the keyword *cohabitation*. Read Wade Horn's article (Fall, 2006) entitled "Fatherhood, Cohabitation, and Marriage" (*AN 24944388*). Horn argues that cohabitative relationships are weak structures in comparison with marriage and that fathers are needed in families in order that children thrive. Do you agree with Horn's thesis? Why or why not?

New York Times Online

Select sociology as the subject and enter *marriage* as the keyword. Look for articles that deal with marriage. Read Betsey Stevenson and Justin Wolfers's article, "Divorced from Reality" (9/29/2007). According to Stevenson and Wolfers, there are a lot of myths floating around in the popular literature about divorce. What are these myths? Is it important for the public to know the facts about divorce? Why?

Link Library
Select sociology as the subject and click on F for family. Next, click on the link for Dysfunctional Families. This website, maintained by Kansas State University, explains what is meant by family dysfunction, indicates how to recognize it, and provides some strategies for dealing with a dysfunctional family. Do you know of anyone who has a dysfunctional family? What impact has this dysfunctional structure had on their behavior?

PRACTICE TEST

MULTIPLE CHOICE QUESTIONS: Select the one best answer for each of the following questions.

1. Extended families are most likely to be found in
   a. hunting and gathering societies.
   b. industrial societies.
   c. agrarian societies.
   d. postindustrial societies.

2. Industrial societies favor the nuclear family because it
   a. allows for geographic mobility.
   b. maintains a large family size.
   c. is dependent on intergenerational support.
   d. is similar to agrarian families.

3. The author suggests hat different stresses and other personal problems may reduce the family to a "______," one that is held together not so much by feelings of warmth and attraction as by outside pressures.
   a. heartless haven
   b. hollow home
   c. empty shell
   d. cavernous divide

4. Today, about ____ percent of American women with children under the age of 18 work outside of the home.
   a. 30
   b. 50
   c. 70
   d. 90

5. Arlie Hochschild's concept of the "second shift" refers to
   a. the second job many families need to make ends meet.
   b. the secondary change that occurred in American families when women entered the workforce.
   c. the economic change associated with an increase in divorce.
   d. the work women do for their families after work.

6. One of the consequences of the difficulties couples encounter in juggling work and family is that
   a. marital happiness often decreases when babies are born.
   b. marital happiness often improves when babies are born.
   c. couples become closer when babies are born.
   d. women find fulfillment when babies are born.

7. Some observers believe that the increasing amount of part-time work helps
   a. women fulfill career goals and family goals.
   b. employers more than employees.
   c. men become more involved in their children's lives.
   d. employers support family values.

8. Much of the differences between black and white families can be attributed to
   a. different values in life.
   b. differences in opportunities and behavior.
   c. different views of sex roles.
   d. less desire to keep the family intact.

9. Divorce and remarriage have become commonplace in American society. In 2005,
   a. half as many couples got divorced as married.
   b. one-third of those who married are now divorced.
   c. two-thirds of those who married are now divorced.
   d. three-quarters of those who married are now divorced.

10. The highest rate of divorce, amounting to about one-third of all divorces, occurs _______ years after marriage
   a. after fifteen
   b. after twenty-five
   c. in the first three
   d. in the first five

11. Which of the following has NOT been advanced as a cause of divorce?
   a. growing community support services for single parents
   b. increased education and employment of women
   c. reformation of divorce laws
   d. loss of functions fulfilled by the family unit

12. There are about 1.2 million divorces in the Untied States each year. Of these, approximately ____ percent involve couples who have one or more children.
   a. 10
   b. 20
   c. 30
   d. 50

13. _____ percent of families in the United States are stepfamilies
   a. Ten
   b. Twenty-five
   c. Fifty
   d. Over 75

14. It is estimated that there are approximately ____ million cohabiting couples in the United States.
   a. 1.5
   b. 3.5
   c. 5
   d. 10

15. The postponement of marriage to later ages results in
    a. higher divorce rates.
    b. better marriages.
    c. a "marriage squeeze" for some women.
    d. a "second shift."

16. The teenage birthrate in the United States is
    a. about the same as other developed countries.
    b. higher than other developed countries.
    c. lower than other developed countries.
    d. higher than it ever been in the last fifty years..

17. The children of gay and lesbian couples
    a. play different games than the children of heterosexual couples.
    b. have lower IQs than the children of heterosexual couples.
    c. have similar likes and dislikes as children of heterosexual couples.
    d. are more likely to be gay.

18. A family in which there is child abuse typically has which of the following characteristics?
    a. Both parents are present.
    b. The family includes four or more children and has received some kind of public assistance within a year of the abuse.
    c. The parents' socioeconomic status and level of education are above average.
    d. The parents are very antiauthoritarian.

19. Several states have taken the lead in passing laws that create ______ marriages, making it more difficult to get a divorce.
    a. seminal
    b. residual
    c. covenant
    d. hybrid

20. Sex education and access to birth control
    a. have increased teenage pregnancy in some European countries.
    b. have received wide support from conservative politicians.
    c. are only effective when supported by family values.
    d. have been shown to reduce rates of teenage pregnancy.

ESSAY QUESTIONS

1. Define and distinguish nuclear, extended, and modified extended families.

2. What has been the impact of women entering the labor force on the nuclear family?

3. What are some of the effects of divorce? Describe in particular the impact on women.

4. Describe differences between white families and black families and factors that could help explain those differences.

5. Discuss factors that are associated with changes in the rates of teenage pregnancy.

ANSWERS TO MULTIPLE CHOICE QUESTIONS

1.	c	11.	a
2.	a	12.	d
3.	c	13.	c
4.	c	14.	b
5.	d	15.	c
6.	a	16.	b
7.	b	17.	c
8.	b	18.	b
9.	a	19.	c
10.	c	20.	d

CHAPTER ELEVEN

Problems of Education

CHAPTER OULINE

I. Sociological Perspectives on Education
   A. Functionalist Approaches
   B. Conflict Approaches
   C. Interactionist Approaches
II. Educational Attainment and Achievement
      1. How U.S. Students Measure Up in International Comparisons
III. Education and Equality: The Issue of Equal Access
   A. Black Students
   B. Hispanic Students
      1. Bilingual/Bicultural Education
      2. Asian Students
   C. Preschool Programs
   D. Desegregation
IV. School Reform: Problems of Institutional Change
   A. School as Bureaucracies
   B. Classroom and School Size
   C. School Choice
      1. Charter Schools
      2. Homeschooling
   D. The Technological Fix
   E. Teacher's Unions
   F. School Violence
V. Social Policy
   A. Educational Conservatism and Back to Basics
      1. Testing for Educational Excellence, or Drill and Kill?
      2. The Texas Miracle
      3. Reading First and Social-Scientific Evaluation
   B. Humanism and Open Education
   C. Access to Higher Education
      1. Privatization of Public Higher Education
   D. Future Prospects
VI. Going Beyond Left and Right
VII. Summary
VIII. Key Terms
IX. Social Problems Online
X. Research Navigator

LEARNING OBJECTIVES

After reading Chapter Eleven you should:

1. Be aware of the many demands placed on the educational system in the United States.

2. Be familiar with the functionalist, conflict, and interactionist approaches to education.
3. Know about issues of equality and equal access to education and how black and Hispanic students are affected by this.
4. Be familiar with preschool programs like Head Start.
5. Know about problems associated with desegregation.
6. Be familiar with patterns in educational attainment today.
7. Be aware of problems associated with reforming schools, including the impact of increasing bureaucratization on policy implementation and how classroom and school size affects education.
8. Know about school choice as a strategy for improving educational performances.
9. Be aware of the push to introduce technology into the classroom.
10. Know how teachers' unions affect school operations.
11. Be aware of violence in the school.
12. Know how social policy impacts the educational institution.
13. Be familiar with conservatism and the back to basics approach.
14. Understand what is meant by a humanistic approach to education.
15. Know about current policy trends in educational access, including community colleges and open admissions programs.

KEY TERMS

educational attainment
educational achievement
human capital
humanism
progressivism
open education

CHAPTER SUMMARY

In democratic nations education is expected to meet many needs and address many social problems. This includes teaching basic skills in literacy, computation, and written expression, as well as preparing professionals and leaders. Additionally, schools are expected to address problems like racism, sexism, and violence. The Bush administration has developed the No Child Left Behind program that develops national achievement tests, encourages failing students to accept tutoring, and punishes schools that fail to raise student test scores to national averages in two years.

Sociological Perspectives on Education

Problems in the educational system are a symptom of social disorganization. Schools are not designed to handle the problems of students from disorganized families. Also, many educational problems stem from deviance from the norms of achievement. Another functionalist approach looks at how educational institutions can be shaped to meet the requirements of changing economics and culture.

There are two main conflict approaches: Marxist and non-Marxist. The Marxist approach stresses the goal of reducing social stratification and increasing equality. The non-Marxist approach is referred to as the value conflict approach, and it focuses on intergroup conflicts that arise out of the desire to defend a group's status in a community. For example, school busing is the source of much conflict.

According to the interactionist perspective, schools label students achievers or underachievers, and those labels follow them forever. Dornbusch's research shows that students label themselves with terms like slacker and nerd to categorize each other. **Table 11-1** summarizes the views and policy recommendations of these three sociological perspectives.

Educational Attainment and Achievement

More American students are finishing high school and going on to college. The gap between blacks and whites has narrowed, but whites still have higher graduation rates than blacks and Hispanics. Minority dropout rates are important as dropouts earn less. About 40 percent eventually return to the educational system. Cutbacks in federally funded assistance put college out of the reach of many.

Achievement is difficult to assess; however, the TIMSS study and some research on declining SAT scores suggest achievement is a problem because U. S. children did not perform as well as comparable children in Asian schools. Other research casts doubt on these findings. In addition, TIMSS found that tracking is more common in the United States than in Germany or Japan. It is difficult to determine whether America's schools are actually failing, but the debate continues.

Education and Equality: The Issue of Equal Access

It is well known that educational attainment is strongly correlated with socioeconomic status. Parents' education and the number and kinds of books at home have an impact as well. One problem with our schools is that many central city schools have fewer resources; Native American and Alaskan Inuit are also affected.

A major factor in the lower educational attainment of blacks than whites is that before WWI, about 90 percent of all blacks in the United States lived in southern states. Southern states spend less on education. In the North, three factors account for differences. Differences in educational levels of parents, high rates of unemployment, and segregation have negatively impacted black academic performance.

Hispanic students are highly concentrated in metropolitan areas. The educational attainment for Hispanic students is lower than the average for all students. Hispanics have experienced language problems, de facto segregation, and poor schools. One technique used to help Hispanic students is bilingual/bicultural education. This is controversial. Some believe that cultural integrity should be maintained, while others advocate immersion. Students from Chinese, Korean, East Indian, and other Asian backgrounds face entirely different problems in U.S. schools.

Head Start and other early education programs have grown in importance. Studies show these to be effective. Head Start would not exist without the pioneering early intervention project in Michigan, known as the Perry Preschool Project. Results of this project showed improved cognitive performance during early childhood; decreased rates of delinquency, crime, use of welfare services, and teen pregnancy; and increased high school and college enrollment rates. Unfortunately, only one in five preschool children in families below the poverty level attends a high-quality preschool program. Early-childhood education programs are considered investments in "human capital."

Efforts to deal with some of these problems have centered on racial desegregation. These efforts began with *Brown v. Board of Education of Topeka, Kansas*. Desegregation slowed in the 1980s. Factors affecting desegregation efforts include the distribution of white and nonwhite populations, and the tendency of middle-class parents to enroll their children in private schools. In 1991, the Supreme Court held that Oklahoma City schools could be permitted to cease busing students. Further, the Reagan administration did not pursue school districts that failed to make progress toward desegregation.

School Reform: Problems of Institutional Change

The primary obstacle to significant changes in the educational system is a built-in tendency to resist change. The nature of schools themselves is a major barrier to change. The maintenance of order and control are major concerns in education, and this leads to the development of elaborate sets of rules and monitoring systems.

Research shows an increase in bureaucratization; this pattern accompanies increases in size and specialization. Schools also have an elaborate system of authority and the many layers make it harder to control the implementation of policies. The typical school district's educational bureaucracy model is illustrated in **Figure 11-5**.

Classroom size is a major issue in school reform. Project Star revealed that smaller classes yield better results. In the United States, average class size is twenty-three; most teachers and administrators believe that seventeen is ideal. Inner-city classrooms may have more than thirty students. Another reform movement calls for reducing school size to decrease impersonality and increase parent and teacher voices in the classroom.

In 2002, the Supreme Court upheld a state run school choice program that allows Cleveland students to attend religious or secular private schools. Research offers little support for the belief that school choice improves performance. Poorer families are less likely than middle-class families to participate in such programs. The Christian Coalition advocates state support for students with a B average or better to attend the college or university of their choice. Two of the major school choice programs today include charter schools and home schooling.

Americans believe in technology. The trend is toward wiring classrooms for computers and the Internet. The Edison Project has drawn attention because of Chris Whittle's claim to be able to transform education. However, most public school teachers only use technology for low-end applications and word processing. More investment needs to be made in human capital, as teachers do not have time to develop curricula around the technological advances being made. Further, there is a growing computer gap between wealthier and poorer school districts.

Teacher's unions also affect school operations. Memberships in the NEA and the NFT have risen. These unions seek to improve the status and material well-being of their members, but have been criticized for opposing policies that seek to improve motivation and competencies. There is a renewed interest in teaching due to publicity about reform, higher salaries, and news of a shortage.

The number of violent victimizations in school has actually declined since 1993. The perception continues that levels are much higher. Reasons for violence include parental failure to supervise, media violence, access to guns, influential outside groups, and low self-esteem. One problem may be that students no longer care about teacher approval. Security devices may deter outside violence but do not convey authority to teachers. A total of 3.3 million children experience domestic violence each year, and it is these individuals who are most likely to commit violent acts against their peers.

Social Policy

Education is most often subjected to institutional change through social policy. School vouchers are one such policy. Changes in property taxes are another; Michigan implemented a new school funding system in 1994 based on sales tax rather than on property tax.

The 1983 report of the National Commission on Excellence in Education (A Nation at Risk) called for longer school hours, more homework, and more discipline. The commission recommended that high schools concentrate on the five new basics: English, math, science, social studies, and computer science. One result of the report is a recommendation for year-round schools and a push for national standards.

The federal No Child Left Behind Act, inspired by what has become called the "Texas Miracle," places heavy stress on achieving its goals through standardized tests in the primary grades. Schools that fall behind can be penalized. Some refer to this approach as "drill and kill." Although support of the goals of greater accountability and higher achievement is strong, state educational leaders are having difficulty funding new programs to meet the federal standards for test results. The centerpiece of the new research-based approach that grew out of the No Child Left Behind legislation was Reading First. By 2007, this program was mired in scandal and charges of widespread corruption.

Humanism, a more liberal approach to education, stresses maximizing self-development for each learner. This movement began with ***Progressivism***, which emphasized vocational training, daily living skills, and a child-centered curriculum. The outgrowth of this was ***open education***, or individualized instruction. Little evidence exists to support this approach.

The community college is assuming a central role in current educational policy. Community colleges are emerging as a primary training and retraining institution, helping people to adapt to rapid economic changes. In other countries, apprenticeship programs are the norm. Privatization and the rising cost of tuition threaten access to state universities. Figures released in 2005 show that taxpayer support for public universities has fallen. The open admission program of CUNY has been successful in helping students make lasting gains in their jobs and incomes. However, more white than minority students take advantage of the program.

Current trends in educational policy include efforts to improve the quality of public school teaching, a longer year in some communities, and school choice. The need to provide more incentives for teachers has been recognized; at the same time, it is agreed that the quality of teachers must be improved. Although more resources are needed to fund education, the prospects are not bright.

Going Beyond Left and Right

Education has become such a fundamental part of our society that it is no wonder there is so much being contested concerning this social institution. There are some tough areas of convergence between people on the left and right sides of the debate over school reform. The need to raise standards is one. Another is the need for greater access to higher education. There does not seem to be much consensus though on how to fund elementary or public colleges and universities.

RESEARCH NAVIGATOR EXERCISES

Content Select

Select the sociology database and enter the keywords *school violence*. Look for studies that focus on the prevalence of school violence or how to prevent it. Look for an FBI Law Enforcement Bulletin on "School Safety" (May, 2007) (*AN 25473028).* In this article, there is a link to the full publication from which the cited data are drawn. You may want to consult this document: http://www.ojp.usdoj.gov/bjs/pub/pdf/iscs06.pdf. Are you surprised by the volume of violent incidents in our nation's schools? What do you think should be done?

New York Times Online

Select the sociology database and enter the keywords *dropout rates*. Read the article "Program to Deter High School Dropouts by Offering College Courses Is Approved" (Oct 24, 2007). Do you think this new program will accomplish the goal of lowering the dropout rate in the state of New York? Why or why not?

Link Library

Use sociology as the subject, and click on E for education. Click on Education, then on the National Center for Education Statistics. On this page, click on Ed Stats at a Glance. Enter "School Crime and Safety" in the SEARCH box. Then, click on "Indicators of School Crime and Safety, 2006." After you have read the report, summarize the key findings in this investigation.

PRACTICE TEST

MULTIPLE CHOICE QUESTIONS: Select the one best answer for each of the following questions.

1. The Bush administration and Congress have developed the program known as ________________, which relies on national achievement tests and punishment of schools that fail to raise student test scores.
   a. No Child Left Behind
   b. It Takes a Village to Raise a Child
   c. Head Start
   d. TIMSS

2. Which theoretical perspective examines how problems in education are symptoms of social disorganization?
   a. functionalist
   b. conflict
   c. interactionist
   d. humanist

3. Which theoretical perspective stresses the importance of reducing social inequality?
   a. functionalist
   b. value conflict
   c. Marxist conflict
   d. humanist

4. The non-Marist version of the conflict perspective is referred to as the ________ approach.
   a. anomie
   b. value conflict
   c. disorganization
   d. mechanical distortion

5. Which theoretical perspective focuses on the consequences of labels like "slacker" and "nerd" for educational outcomes?
   a. functionalist
   b. conflict
   c. interactionist
   d. humanist

6. Which of the following groups has experienced inadequate education and problems with access to high-quality education?
   a. blacks
   b. Hispanics
   c. Native Americans
   d. all of the above

7. The Third International Mathematics and Science Study found
   a. American children outperformed comparable Asian children.
   b. Asian children outperformed comparable American children.
   c. tracking is more common in Japan than in the United States.
   d. American parents demand more from their children than Asian parents.

8. Which of the following is true for black students?
   a. They are disproportionately concentrated in the Northeast.
   b. They have closed the education gap in the North.
   c. They face the consequences of segregation which tends to increase disparities in education.
   d. They have closed the education gap in the South.

9. Which of the following is true for Hispanic students?
   a. They have higher educational attainment levels than blacks.
   b. They have not had to deal with de facto segregation, whereas blacks have.
   c. They have been helped by the United States' widespread acceptance of bilingual/bicultural programs.
   d. None of the above are true.

10. The Perry Preschool Project found that high-quality preschool education
   a. improved cognitive performance in early childhood.
   b. improved scholastic achievement during school years.
   c. decreased delinquency and crime rates.
   d. All of the above are true.

11. Research shows that _____ preschool children in families below the poverty line attends a high-quality preschool program.
   a. 1 in 2 c. 1 in 4
   b. 1 in 3 d. 1 in 5

12. Desegregation effectively began with the U.S. Supreme Court's decision in *Brown v. the Board of Education of Topeka, Kansas* in
   a. 1928. c. 1965.
   b. 1954. d. 1975.

13. Project _______ was a longitudinal study conducted in Tennessee schools which found that smaller classes yield better results.
   a. Star c. Galaxy
   b. Zenith d. Milky Way

14. In the United States, the average primary level classroom size is ______.
   a. 13 c. 23
   b. 17 d. 33

15. The belief that introducing computers into the classroom and providing Internet access will improve educational outcomes is known as the
   a. Digital Divide.
   b. Technological Fix.
   c. E-Solution.
   d. Compu-Fix.

16. Which of the following is NOT cited as a possible cause of school violence by social scientists?
   a. failure of parents to supervise their children
   b. the impact of outsider groups
   c. low self-esteem brought on by social isolation
   d. after-school activities, like school sports

17. Of all American institutions, which of the following is most subject to intentional change through social policy?
   a. family c. legal
   b. education d. religion

18. The National Commission on Excellence in Education called for which of the following?
  a. more individual choice for students
  b. self-paced instruction
  c. less homework
  d. longer school hours

19. ________ is an intellectual tradition that suggests the basic aim of education is to promote the maximum self-development of each individual learner, paying specific attention to differences among individuals' interests, needs, abilities, and values.
  a. Humanism
  b. Progressivism
  c. Positivism
  d. Intersubjectivism

20. ___________ continue to be the primary training and retraining institutions, thereby helping people to adapt to rapid economic changes.
  a. Online schools
  b. Community colleges
  c. Four-year colleges
  d. Private universities

ESSAY QUESTIONS

1. Compare and contrast the major theoretical perspectives on education.

2. Discuss the differences in educational attainment among black, Hispanic, and white students. Be sure to note reasons for the differences.

3. Discuss why schools are difficult to reform.

4. Describe current patterns in school violence; be sure to note factors that make school violence more likely.

5. What is the back to basics movement? What are the issues in the fight over establishing national standards?

ANSWERS TO MULTIPLE CHOICE QUESTIONS

1.	a	11.	d
2.	a	12.	b
3.	c	13.	a
4.	b	14.	c
5.	c	15.	b
6.	d	16.	d
7.	b	17.	b
8.	c	18.	d
9.	d	19.	a
10.	d	20.	b

CHAPTER TWELVE

Problems of Work and the Economy

CHAPTER OUTLINE

I. The American Free-Enterprise System: Key Trends
II. Global Markets and Corporate Power
  A. Multinational Corporations
  B. Global Factory, Global Sweat Shops
III. Effects on American Workers
  A. From Manufacturing to Services
  B. Women in the Global Labor Market
  C. Technology and Specialization
    1. Technology
    2. Specialization
IV. Problem Aspects of Work
  A. The Changing Nature of Employment
    1. Insecurity about Declines in "Good Jobs"
    2. Unemployment
    3. The Intermittently and Chronically Unemployed
    4. Frictional Unemployment and Permanent Displacement
    5. The "Invisible" Unemployed and the "Discouraged" Worker
    6. Consequences of Unemployment
  B. Job Stress
  C. Alienation
  D. Occupational Safety and Health
V. Consumers and Credit
  A. Problems of Debt Entanglement
  B. Corporate Crime and Business Failure
VI. Social Policy
  A. Future Prospects
VII. Going Beyond Left and Right
VIII. Summary
IX. Key Terms
X. Social Problems Online
XI. Research Navigator

LEARNING OBJECTIVES

After reading Chapter Twelve you should:

1. Know the elements of the American free enterprise system, including the definitions for capitalism, markets, capital, entrepreneur, corporation, and limited liability.
2. Know the relationship between global markets and corporate power; be familiar with the concept of the multinational corporation.
3. Know how multinational corporations have affected American workers.

4. Be familiar with the process of shifting from a manufacturing to a service economy.
5. Know about the role of women in the global labor market.
6. Know about the link between technology and specialization.
7. Be familiar with the problem aspects of work, including computers in the workplace, job insecurity and unemployment, job stress, and alienation.
8. Be able to describe and discuss frictional unemployment, permanent displacement, the invisible unemployed, and discouraged workers.
9. Be familiar with occupational health and safety issues.
10. Know about consumerism and credit problems.
11. Understand the phenomenon of corporate crime, and what gave rise to the Enron debacle.
12. Understand current issues in social policy as they relate to the economy.

KEY TERMS

capitalism
markets
capital
entrepreneur
limited liability
economic globalization
multinational corporations
outsourcing
flexitime
alienation

CHAPTER SUMMARY

The American Free-Enterprise System: Key Trends

The U.S. economy remains perhaps the strongest on earth, but its institutions are going through rapid and dramatic changes that can be grouped into a few master trends: globalization of markets and the rise of major multinational corporations, growth in service-sector jobs and the export of manufacturing jobs, increasing reliance of families on the incomes of multiple workers, and increased reliance on innovations in technology and specialization to increase the productivity and competitive of companies and their employees.

The American free-enterprise system is based on ***capitalism***, a form of economy in which the central institutions are ***markets***, which regulate the worldwide flow of an almost infinite array of goods and services. In a pure free-enterprise system, markets are regulated by supply and demand. Almost all markets in the world have some degree of government regulation; e.g., buyer protection from unsafe products, regulation of imports, and monopoly prevention.

Capital refers to equipment and to hourly and salaried labor that is used by capitalists to make a profit. In a pure form of free enterprise, the investor, who tries to make as much profit as possible without regulation, assumes all risk. ***Entrepreneurs*** are capitalists who create new business ventures.

One way to avoid risk is to form a corporation because they provide limited liability for debt to the owners and stockholders. ***Limited liability*** then is the idea that members of a corporation cannot be held accountable for its debts; they lose only the money they invest and so personal assets cannot be seized to pay the corporation's debts.

Global Markets and Corporate Power

Corporations are major players in the process of ***economic globalization***, or the tendency for goods and services to be produced in one nation and consumed in another. Many corporations are ***multinational corporations***, meaning that they have headquarters in one nation, but pursue business and profits in others. Such companies have vast wealth that often exceeds that of many countries. Multinationals can move operations quickly from one location to the next, often harming workers in the process. Increasingly the term multinational is used to emphasize the fact that these corporations operate outside national boundaries almost as if they were nations unto themselves. Two kinds of technology are key to the global factory: high-speed transportation and component production. The former allows companies to get raw materials, finished products, etc., anywhere in the world; the second allows them to take advantage of cheap labor.

The growth of multinational corporations has led to a decline in American manufacturing jobs. Over the last 100 years, agricultural and industrial jobs have declined in number, while white-collar jobs have increased in number. One benefit of this shift is a reduction in the number of on-the-job deaths. On the other hand, union memberships have declined. Unions are associated with higher wages and better health benefits.

Critics of multinationals have condemned ***outsourcing***, or locating plants that produce goods for American markets in third-world nations where the firm can take advantage of lower wage rates. This has moved industrial jobs from the United States to other countries. A recent trend shows that some multinationals from other countries are increasing their investments here, but tend to resist union contracts.

Multinationals have been criticized for using child labor to keep costs down. Critics of this practice believe that the United States should apply trade sanctions to punish this practice. Representatives of countries where these practices take place argue that worker rights would actually hamper economic development in their countries, as cheap labor is one of the few advantages their countries have in the global market.

Effects on American Workers

In the 1970s and 1980s, U.S. plants, factories, mills, and other industrial facilities suffered as capital was diverted abroad. Many were closed, and the cities they were located in suffered severe economic and social upheavals. The biggest losers in the decline of manufacturing have been industrial cities in the Midwest and Northeast.

Over the past generation, there have been three major changes in the American labor force. First was the shift from manufacturing to service employment. Second was the increase of women in the workforce. Third was the emergence of new technologies.

The transition of the economy from agriculture to industry can be gauged by changes in the workforce. In 1900, 27 percent of the total workforce consisted of farm workers and 18 percent of white-collar workers. By 2007, only about 2.2 percent of the total workforce consisted of farm, forestry, and fishing workers; 60 percent consisted of white-collar workers. White-collar workers, professional, managerial, clerical, and sales personnel are the largest occupational category in the nation, surpassing the blue-collar groups since 1956.

Most new white-collar jobs are professional and clerical. The number of clerical personnel has increased by 500 percent since 1900, and now accounts for about 17 percent of all employed people. Blue-collar workers have experienced many changes, including a decline in the number of unskilled laborers. The shift to a service economy has brought many changes, including a decline in the number of accidents and deaths on the job. In 1960, the accidental death rate at work was 21 per 100,000 workers. By 2000, the rate declined to 4 per 100,000 workers. Mining and agriculture remain the most dangerous jobs, with accidental death rates of 30 percent and 20 percent, respectively. The death rate for service jobs is 2 per 100,000.

Another aspect of the shift from manufacturing to service jobs is the previously mentioned decline in union membership. In 1960, about 27 percent of workers were members of unions; today the figure is 9 percent. Contingent work, i.e., work that is not based on written employment contracts and regular hours, is also increasing.

The federal government defines the labor force as all people 16 years of age or over who worked one hour for pay during one survey week, plus those who did not work during the survey week, do not have a job, but are looking for one. The most significant trend in the labor force is the inclusion of women and the exclusion of older men.

A century ago, women and men rarely did the same work. Married women were expected to stay at home. Between 1940 and 1990, the proportion of women in the labor force rose by 10 percentage points per decade. The proportion of married women with their spouse who work is 71.2 percent. For women with other marital statuses, it is almost 79 percent. Over 80 percent of women who have bachelor's degrees are in the labor force.

The number of people in the labor force has increased. In 1970, there were 78 million men and women in the labor force. Today, there are more than 130 million; over 40 percent of these are women. About 6 percent of men and women hold more than one job; 31 percent of these do so to pay regular household bills. Twenty-one million worked less than 35 hours per week in 1998 and averaged about 21 hours per week. The majority of part-time workers are women. About 6.6 million men and women say they work part time because of school; 5.5 million say they work part time because of family obligations, including problems with child care. Good jobs remain incompatible with child-rearing roles. When women go to work, they buy child-care services and more takeout food and other services, all of which drive economic growth but also increase stratification.

Economic growth of the 1990s was fueled by the rise of new technologies, including computers, telecommunications, biotechnologies, and e-commerce. Between 1993 and 1998, the percentage of workers who use computers in their jobs increased from 46 percent to 50 percent, which translated into an additional 12.5 million computer users. Computers and telecommunications have created new Internet-related businesses, such as Amazon.com and eBay. This kind of technology has increased the number of self-employed people. In 2006, over 10 million people reported that they were self-employed. Researchers Aronowitz and DiFazio argue that technology may create a jobless future for millions; others who say that the U.S. economy has continued to produce new jobs at all skill levels critique this view.

This long-term trend began long before the advent of computers. As the number of goods and services increases, so does specialization. The Department of Labor lists more than 22,000 jobs; there were 325 listed in the 1850 Census. Specialization has important implications. First, those trained only for a single, narrow job and who lose it may have difficulty in finding another like it. Second, these workers may experience dissatisfaction because they are unable to use more than minor skills or abilities. Third, high-level managers experience problems of coordination and cooperation.

Problem Aspects of Work

Some negative consequences of computers in the workplace include a feeling of stress, over-supervision, and excessive discipline. Computer controls also affect the structure of the organization. Computer-based operations require a separate data processing staff, whose job it is to provide efficient means of production. People with high status in the organization but no technical expertise must cooperate with the technical experts, who have no supervisory authority. This relationship is unique to modern organizations.

Computer technologies have also eliminated jobs; e.g., drafting and computers can do design tasks in architecture. Workers who remain are anxious that new technologies will eliminate their jobs as well. Work will probably become more demanding and precise; this will increase the need for a highly educated workforce. There will be more job insecurity and job stress.

Between 2000 and 2002, unemployment rates increased sharply as a result of a sharp downturn in the economy and the lingering effects of a weak world economy and the September 11, 2001, terrorist attacks. In the past, economic downturns produced high levels of unemployment among blue-collar workers, but the end of the high-tech investment bubble and the declines in aerospace and other high-tech industries have caused insecurity in the ranks of managers and skilled professionals. Unemployment rates decreased for all workers between 1992 and 2000, but rose dramatically between 2000 and 2002. Since 2001, managers and professionals have spent more time unemployed than they did during the boom years.

A striking feature of the years from 2000 to 2006 was relatively high employment rates and consistently low unemployment. There is ongoing insecurity, however, regarding declines in "good jobs." Even when the unemployment rate is low, many people are unemployed for part of the year (intermittently unemployed) and others are underemployed. More serious is the problem of chronic unemployment. In general, the unemployment rate for blacks and other minority groups is twice as high as the rate for whites.

Many workers undergo short spells of unemployment; they may be temporarily laid off from a factory job or may leave one job to search for one that is better. This is called frictional unemployment because it is a normal consequence of labor force mobility or brief economic changes in local labor markets. However, much unemployment results in permanent displacement of workers.

Official unemployment data do not include those who are able to work but who are not actively seeking work during the survey week. Official data also do not adequately reflect those who are underemployed with part-time jobs. "Invisible" unemployment becomes more problematic during economic recessions. It is estimated that during the recession of the early 1990s, about one million people dropped out of the labor force. More "discouraged workers" appeared.

Those who are unemployed tend to be socially isolated. Research by Braginsky and Braginsky on high-status unemployed men showed that they experienced a "social transformation" in which they became depressed, felt ashamed, and avoided friends. Many of those who did find new jobs did not fully recover their self-esteem. As more women enter the labor force, the consequences of unemployment for them have become more important, especially for single mothers, the divorced, and the separated. The single greatest reason women go on welfare is the "double jeopardy" situation of loss of spouse and loss of job.

As more people work multiple jobs, are employed on a contingent basis, or experience the sometimes frantic environment of high-tech companies, their physical and mental lives are often negatively affected. A 1999 survey by the National Institute for Occupational Safety and Health found that job stress was reaching alarming levels. According to NIOSH, stress can be alleviated by ensuring that workloads are appropriate for workers' capabilities, clearly defining worker roles, improving communication, providing opportunities for interaction, and establishing work schedules that are compatible with other life responsibilities.

The concept of ***flextime***, or sliding work hours, is very appealing to workers; some workers stay in jobs they dislike because of flextime. However, it is more usual for American and European workers to fear displacement and experience increased demand for longer hours than to have flexibility. Critics of the automated, postindustrial society argue that these conditions are likely to cause new outbreaks of industrial strife and stimulate workers to form unions. Workers who lose the capacity to express themselves in their work will experience ***alienation***.

Occupational health remains a serious problem. Mining, agriculture, forestry, fishing, transportation, and construction have the highest fatality rates. Job-related diseases take the lives of at least 100,000 Americans each year. The greatest health hazards come from the chemicals industry. Chemicals can cause cancer, and workers who are exposed to certain chemicals have an unusually high rate of malignancies. That more workers do not complain about working conditions may have to do with their fear of unemployment and their high levels of indebtedness.

Consumers and Credit

The United States is a consumer economy; corporations depend on the disposable income of consumers. A consumer society requires a large middle and upper class with enough leisure time to enjoy the use of many goods and services. Drawbacks to a consumer economy include the dominance of large corporations and franchise operations and unplanned spread of shopping malls.

The most serious flaw of a consumer society is that it requires the ready availability of credit. Large-scale production of consumer goods depends on a steady flow of profits, which in turn requires that purchases be made constantly, not just when the consumer has a windfall or has accumulated enough money.

Since the 1950s, the United States has been transformed from a cash to a credit society. Outstanding installment debt was $29 billion in 1955; it has risen to more than $700 billion today. While this has helped the economy to grow, it has also increased bankruptcy and debt entanglement. Research shows that half of all bankruptcies are due to financial failure on the part of average homeowners, particularly female heads of households. A study of bankruptcy filing showed that less than 2 percent were credit card "junkies"; 10 percent made risky investments; most were homeowners who could no longer pay their debts because of family dissolution or medical emergencies.

The failure of Enron, followed by revelations of wrongdoing among other large corporations, has created a major economic crisis for American corporations. Between 1999 and 2001, senior executives and directors of major corporations siphoned off about $5 billion in salary, bonuses, and the proceeds from sales of stock and stock options, knowing that their companies were about to lose much of their value. Many analysts blame the system of corporate compensation, which made it possible for executives to receive huge sums of money, even though they knew that their companies' earnings records were being falsified.

Social Policy

As a result of terrorism, the United States is once again spending heavily on the military. Globalization led to the passage of NAFTA in 1993, and the emergence of the European Union in the 1990s. NAFTA is intended to move the nations of North America closer to free trade. Congress recently voted to grant Most Favored Nation trading status to China; pro-labor groups oppose this. In 2005, Congress passed the Sarbanes-Oxley bill, which imposes strict reporting requirements on corporate leaders and members of corporate boards.

In the future, the U.S. administration, whether Democratic or Republican, is likely to push for more free trade and fewer international tariffs. In a recession, welfare reform in the absence of job-creating strategies is likely to cause many economic and social hardships.

Going Beyond Left and Right

On the right there is a tendency to favor social policies that cost as little as possible, rely on the forces of supply and demand, and insist on individual initiatives. On the left, there is a tendency to support policies that use the power of government to shape economic outcomes. In a recession, it is likely that liberals and conservatives will reach a compromise on job creation strategies.

RESEARCH NAVIGATOR EXERCISES

ContentSelect

Use the finance and economics database and enter the keywords *corporate scandal.* The text mentions congressional passage of the Sarbanes-Oxley bill, which imposes strict reporting requirements on corporate leaders and members of corporate boards. Also mentioned is the fact that in 2005, business lobbyists were complaining that the law was imposing new and costly requirements on business. Read the December,2006 article by Alex Pollack on how this legislation needs "fixing" (*AN 23287137*). Where do you stand on the issues? How do you think your views are a reflection of either "left" or "right"?

New York Times Online
Use sociology as the subject and enter the keyword *corporate malfeasance*. Look for articles that deal with this topic. Read Paul Krugman's article (10/7/07), "Enron's Second Coming?" Do you agree or disagree with Mr. Krugman's assessment? What are your views on American corporate CEOs receiving multimillion dollar bonuses and other incentives, even after these officials have been shown to have failed in their efforts and/or have been suspected of malfeasance?

Link Library
Use sociology as the subject and click on U for unemployment. Look for the link to the Department of Labor. Look at unemployment over time by clicking on "Where can I find unemployment rates for previous years?" in the "People Are Asking" section. Note that there is considerable fluctuation in the unemployment rate. Why do you think that unemployment rates never dipped as low in the 1990s as they did during the 1950s? Next, go back to the home page for the Department of Labor and look for data that will provide you with work experience of the population. Look at the extent of unemployment by sex. Notice that the unemployment rates are sometimes higher for men than for women. Speculate on the reasons for this.

PRACTICE TEST

MULTIPLE CHOICE QUESTIONS: Select the one best answer for each question below.

1. ________ are the central institutions of capitalism that serve to regulate the worldwide flow of goods and services.
   a. Markets
   b. Entrepreneurs
   c. Monopolies
   d. Labor pools

2. A ________ is a capitalist who creates new business ventures.
   a. A CEO
   b. An investor
   c. A broker
   d. An entrepreneur

3. ________ refers to the growing tendency for goods and services to be produced in one nation and consumed in another.
   a. Limited liability
   b. Economic globalization
   c. Multinationalism
   d. Monopoly

4. __________ corporations have their headquarters in one country but pursue business activities and profits in one or more foreign nations.
   a. Multinational
   b. Global
   c. Unilateral
   d. Transnational

5. ___________ refers to locating plants that produce goods for American markets in less developed nations where the firm can take advantage of lower wage rates.
   a. Globalization
   b. Outsourcing
   c. Transnationalism
   d. Multinationalism

6. In 1960, over 28 percent of all U.S. workers were employed in manufacturing jobs. Today, this figure is about
   a. the same.
   b. 22 percent.
   c. 11 percent.
   d. 4 percent.

7. Which of the following currently represents the largest occupational category in the nation?
   a. white-collar workers
   b. farm workers
   c. forestry workers
   d. factory workers

8. Which of the following has occurred as a result of the shift from a manufacturing to a service economy?
   a. The number of accidents and on-the-job deaths has declined.
   b. Union membership has declined.
   c. Contingent work has increased.
   d. all of the above

9. The proportion of married women living with their spouse who work is currently about _______ percent.
   a. 41.3
   b. 71.2
   c. 81.9
   d. 91.7

10. In 2006, about __________ percent of women worked regularly with computers, far above the national average.
   a. 30
   b. 40
   c. 50
   d. 60

11. Specialization has which of the following consequences?
    a. Those who are trained for a single job and who lose it may have difficulty finding another like it.
    b. Managers are better able to coordinate worker activities and to get their cooperation.
    c. It tends to increase worker satisfaction.
    d. all of the above

12. Many workers undergo short periods of unemployment, and they may temporarily be laid off from one job or leave one to look for another. This is called _________ unemployment.
    a. frictional
    b. chronic
    c. intermittent
    d. invisible

13. The single greatest reason women go on welfare is the double jeopardy situation of
    a. loss of spouse and loss of job.
    b. loss of child and loss of job.
    c. loss of spouse and loss of child.
    d. none of the above

14. The concept of _____, or sliding work hours, is very appealing to workers.
    a. floating time
    b. rotating shifts
    c. flextime
    d. job-sharing

15. Workers who lose the capacity to express themselves in their work will experience ________.
    a. mechanicalization
    b. McDonaldization
    c. anomie
    d. alienation

16. About what percent of employees who are killed on the job are men?
    a. 50
    b. 60
    c. 80
    d. 90

17. Outstanding installment debt was $29 billion in 1955; it is _________ billion today.
    a. $400
    b. $500
    c. $700
    d. $900

18. Research shows that _______ percent of all bankruptcies are attributed to "credit card junkies."
    a. 50
    b. 2
    c. 80
    d. 25

19. ________ is intended to move the nations of North America closer to free trade.
   a. AFL-CIO
   b. NAFTA
   c. NATO
   d. DOL

20. Congress recently granted Most Favored Nation status to which country?
   a. China
   b. India
   c. Pakistan
   d. South Africa

ESSAY QUESTIONS

1. Discuss the major characteristics of the American free-enterprise system.

2. Discuss the role of women in the global labor market.

3. Explain the importance of the multinational corporation both in America and abroad.

4. Describe the various problem aspects of work, including job insecurity, job stress, alienation, unemployment, and occupational safety and health.

5. Discuss the problem of corporate crime and its link to business failure.

ANSWERS TO MULTIPLE CHOICE QUESTIONS

1.	a	11.	a
2.	d	12.	a
3.	b	13.	a
4.	a	14.	c
5.	a	15.	d
6.	c	16.	d
7.	a	17.	c
8.	d	18.	b
9.	b	19.	b
10.	d	20.	a

CHAPTER THIRTEEN

Urban Problems

CHAPTER OUTLINE

I. An Urbanizing World
II. The American City
  A. Urban Growth and Social Problems
  B. Antiurban Bias
  C. The Composition of Urban Populations
    1. Minority Migration
    2. Voluntary and Involuntary Segregation
    3. Muslim Newcomers in U.S. Cities
III. Theories of Urbanism
  A. Wirth's Theory
  B. Compositionalism
  C. Subcultural Theory
  D. Critical Urban Theory and the Los Angeles School
IV. Metropolitan Growth
  A. Rural Depopulation and Its Consequences
  B. The Transportation Boom
    1. Edge Cities
  C. The Impact of Suburban Growth
V. Problems of Cities
  A. Decentralization
  B. Relocation of Manufacturing
  C. Financial Problems
  D. Government
VI. Shelter Poverty, Homelessness, and Neighborhood Distress
  A. Shelter Poverty
  B. Homelessness
  C. Distressed Neighborhoods
VII. Social Policy
  A. Housing
  B. Homelessness
  C. Future Prospects
VIII. Going Beyond Left and Right
IX. Summary
X. Key Terms
XI. Social Problems Online
XII. Research Navigator

LEARNING OBJECTIVES

After reading Chapter Thirteen you should:

1. Be familiar with some of the social problems that are concentrated in the city.

2. Know how to define terms like "urban population," "urbanized area," "rural area," and "metropolitan region."
3. Be able to discuss the urban revolution as a worldwide phenomenon.
4. Be able to describe the American city in terms of growth patterns over time, urban growth and social problems, antiurban bias, the composition of urban populations, including voluntary and involuntary segregation.
5. Be able to discuss problems of residential segregation.
6. Be able to describe and discuss the major theories of urbanism, including Wirth's theory, Gans's Compositionalism, Fischer's Subcultural theory, and Critical Urban theory.
7. Be familiar with the major patterns of metropolitan growth, including rural depopulation and the categories used by the Census Bureau to define the urban population (CMSA, MSA, PMSA).
8. Know how large urban areas impact the environment.
9. Be familiar with the transportation boom, and changes in car ownership over time.
10. Be able to describe the impact of suburban growth.
11. Be familiar with problems of the cities, including decentralization, relocation of manufacturing, financial problems, and governments.
12. Be able to discuss issues concerning shelter poverty, homelessness, and neighborhood distress.
13. Understand the social policy implications of diverting funds to pay for terrorism and tax cuts on homelessness and shelter poverty and other problems

KEY TERMS

rural
urban
urban population
urbanized area
urbanism
metropolitan districts
consolidated metropolitan statistical area (CMSA)
primary metropolitan statistical areas (PMSAs)
metropolitan statistical areas (MSAs)
megalopolis
decentralization
neighborhood distress
census tracts

CHAPTER SUMMARY

The U.S. Bureau of the Census defines the ***urban population*** as all persons living in places with 2,500 or more inhabitants that are legally incorporated as cities, villages, boroughs, and towns. ***Rural*** is a term referring to an area not classified as urban. ***Urban*** refers to densely settled cities or towns. An **urbanized area** is one or more places and the adjacent densely settled surrounding area that together have a minimum population of 50,000 persons. ***Urbanism*** refers to a way of life that is dependent on industry, mass communication, a mobile population, and mass consumer markets.

An Urbanizing World

The urban revolution is a worldwide phenomenon, as can be seen in the changing ranking of cities. The New York metro area was the largest in the world in 1950; it will be in eleventh place by 2015. In the developing world, people are leaving rural villages to seek their futures in cities. Although the rural-urban transformation was mostly completed in Europe and North America before 1975, it is now underway in Latin America, China, and Africa. **Figure 13-1** highlights the shift toward a predominately urban world.

Rapid urban growth presents major problems for developing nations, which are still struggling with rural poverty. Urban populations depend on investments in infrastructure (water, electricity, sewage, communication); cities can provide opportunities for some, but poverty for others. For example, India has more than 3,000 cities and towns but only eight have sewage treatment plants. World Resources Institutes estimate that 90 percent of the raw sewage from urban areas in developing nations is seeping into streams and oceans. By 2010, 1.4 billion will not have safe water to drink.

The American City

Until the nineteenth century, the United States was an agrarian society; the few existing cities were market towns. Efficient transportation and communication and the effects of industrialization caused the bulk of urban growth. Cities expanded vertically and horizontally due to the use of cast iron in construction, horse-drawn buses, railroads, and telegraphs. Growth presented special problems, and matters of mutual concern arose, e.g., lighting, fire protection, the care of streets, crime prevention, sewage disposal, water, community health, and marketing facilities.

In the twentieth century, adequate water and waste supply systems were developed. Prior to that cities had high death rates. Antiurban sentiment has become a theme in American culture, and it evident in literature as well (e.g., consider references to cities like Sodom and Gomorrah; "Gay Paree"). Recently, the spread of AIDS and addictive drugs like crack have reinforced the negative image of the city. Cities are also viewed as "temporary" places. Polls show that inner cities are viewed negatively. A consequence of this is the growth of the suburb.

The majority of Americans live in large metropolitan areas. Urban life gives rise to subculture, social institutions, and personality traits that are not found in rural settings. Today's cities are largely populated by descendents of rural Americans and immigrants from other countries who came in search of opportunities. Foreign immigrants tended to intermarry and disperse; blacks settled in neighborhoods that quickly became and remained all black, creating cities within cities. Many U.S. cities have seen a continual influx of foreign immigrants over the past four decades. Miami, New York, Los Angeles, and Houston now have large concentrations of immigrants.

Residential segregation may be voluntary, as when people choose to live with others similar to them. It may be involuntary, as when people are forced by social or economic circumstances to live in specific areas of the city. Today, most blacks and other minorities are largely involuntarily segregated; within this there is income segregation. No other population has experienced such persistent residential segregation.

Studies of segregation patterns reveal only a slight change in the mean segregation index since 1970. For most city dwellers, residential segregation means a limited choice of lifestyles. Douglas Massey argues that residential segregation of African Americans contributes to unemployment, educational inequality, high rates of criminal victimization, and drug addiction. He argues for stronger enforcement of the Fair Housing Act. Segregation patterns for the period 1980-2000 are summarized in **Table 13-1**.

People of Muslim background from North Africa, the Middle East, Iran, and South Asia constitute a relatively small minority in the United States. Eighty percent of Muslims in the United States live in metropolitan areas in Los Angeles, New York-New Jersey, Chicago, and Detroit.

Theories of Urbanization

The basic argument of Louis Wirth's theory is that cities increase the incidence of both social and personality disorders. Psychic overload is created by intense, multiple stimuli; this leads to an increase in isolation, aloofness, irritation, and anxiety. Urbanization also produces economic processes of competitiveness and specialization. People assume many roles, and this weakens social bonds. When social bonds are weakened, anomie results. Other ways to control behavior must be devised.

Herbert Gans challenges Wirth's theory. His book *The Urban Villagers* showed that many families were deeply committed to a life within the neighborhood. *Compositionalists* believe that economic position, cultural characteristics, and marital and family status are the determinants of personal behavior. This is more important than the size or density of the community at large.

Fisher's theory agrees that cities produce major social psychological effects because cities foster new groups. These new groups (subcultures) have their own norms and social institutions (e.g., gay communities). Fisher believes that urbanization intensifies subcultures.

Mike Davis, the most widely known member of the Los Angeles School of critical urban theory, is critical of the disregard that rich owners of real estate have for environmental consequences. He emphasizes the extremes of wealth, political conservatism, and dependence on cars and subsidies for highway construction.

In the twentieth century, migration has become inter-metropolitan. In 1910, the U.S. Census Bureau identified twenty-five ***metropolitan districts***. The term was used to assist in measurement of urban populations which could not be contained within traditional urban political boundaries. Since 1938, the U.S. Census Bureau has defined the urban population according to residence in three categories of urban settlements.

The largest is the CMSA, or ***consolidated metropolitan statistical area***. This is a large metropolitan complex within which are recognized subcenters that may themselves have large core areas, called ***primary metropolitan statistical areas***, or PMSAs. ***Metropolitan statistical areas*** (MSAs) have a large urban nucleus (a city of 500,000) and surrounding communities that are linked to it through economic and social activities. Metropolitan and urban areas differ from each other in that the urban area contains a large population within a limited area, while the metropolitan area contains several urban communities located in close proximity to each other.

There has been dramatic growth in the South and West in contrast to the Midwest and Northeast. Although they are not growing rapidly, metropolitan regions in the Northeast remain the largest on the continent; such large areas have been termed a ***megalopolis***. These large areas have large-scale effects on the environment, including acid rain, pollution, and water shortages, as well as depopulation of rural areas. Unlike the U.S., the leading nations of Western Europe have made investments in rail transport, high-speed trains, and improved bus transportation.

Ancient and medieval cities had to be compact because of primitive communication and transportation facilities. By 1870, horse-drawn streetcars allowed people to live as much as 5 miles away from their business. In the 1880s and 1890s, electric trolley cars extended this distance to 10 miles. Rapid transit electric trains doubled this. Commuter railways allowed more people to move to the suburbs. Convenience goods and service businesses followed. By the 1930s, the automobile made suburban development a major factor in economics, politics, and social life. Motor vehicle registration was 8,000 in 1900; in 1930, it was 26,352,000. In the 1980s and 1990s, urban growth entered a new stage with the emergence of ***edge cities***, or large urban clusters that attract businesses and shopping, but little else.

Public policy has increased suburbanization. It is easier to buy homes in the suburbs than the cities, and there are more federal funds for home ownership than for rented housing. Public housing is plagued by crime and tends to keep low-income people in the city. Businesses have left the city, which erodes the tax base. This makes renovation of the city more difficult and increases the percentage of slums.

Problems of Cities

Decentralization refers to middle and upper class flight to the suburbs; an influx of poor minority groups, the chronically unemployed and the aged; the flight of commerce and industry; disparity between residents' job skills and job requirements; and influx of suburban dwellers who use public utilities but don't pay for their upkeep. When affluent households leave, new populations often arrive from other countries. The 2000 census confirmed that the fastest-growing urban communities are on the fringes of metropolitan areas.

Manufacturers have relocated to suburban areas because of cheaper transportation and freight costs. While some new businesses have taken their place, the percentage of white-collar jobs has increased more in the suburbs. High-tech manufacturing areas tend to locate near major universities. High-tech firms have created new jobs, but have also contributed to higher housing costs, which displaces lower-income residents.

Property assessments are the primary source of tax revenues for city governments. The exodus to the suburbs has eroded the real estate tax base of most central cities. As lower-income residents become more concentrated in the inner cities, there is more need for welfare and other programs.

The infrastructure, or physical facilities, of many cities are deteriorating and financial problems preclude repairs. Natural disasters in the 1990s (flooding, earthquakes, fires, and hurricanes) added to the burden of financing the repair and maintenance of urban infrastructure.

A major cause of problems in cities is an inequitable distribution of economic resources and costs of public service between the cities and higher levels of government. Of every $100 collected in taxes, the U.S. government spends about $18 on national defense, $23 on social security, $14 on income security, and $20 on interest on the national debt. It spends less than $1 to run the federal government, $8 on health care and research, $2 on transportation, and a little over $1 on criminal justice assistance to the states.

Social scientists have pointed out that regardless of political boundaries, a metropolitan area is a single economic entity with an integrated labor market, unified transportation system, and a set of interrelated housing markets. Dividing this entity into separate local economies results in inefficiency and duplication of services. Discrepancies between municipal boundaries and social needs can have dire consequences, as in the case of East St. Louis.

Shelter Poverty, Homelessness, and Neighborhood Distress

The majority of America's poor live in substandard, deteriorated housing that has been rejected by people who can afford better. This is especially true of minority groups who inhabit substandard housing either because they can't afford better or because discrimination keeps them where they are. While shelter poverty may affect affluent families impacted by unemployment, it mainly affects those at or near the poverty level.

Urban renewal projects often do little more than displace the poor. Federal housing policy prevents the working poor from living there, so only the very poor are there. The poor are also segregated because affluent communities oppose low-income housing in their neighborhoods.

People who cannot afford rent may become homeless. *Gentrification*, the return of affluent, single people and childless couples to selected central city neighborhoods, also forces poor people out. If unable to find housing, they may end up homeless. There have always been homeless groups in the United States; however, today's homeless people are a more serious problem because they are more numerous and diverse. They place a heavy burden on public and private shelters.

Neighborhood distress has been increasing due to middle class flight to the suburbs. For analytical purposes, census tracts are equivalent to urban neighborhoods. ***Census tracts*** are areas that are relatively homogenous in population, SES, and living conditions. According to social scientists such as Paul Jargoswky, severely distressed neighborhoods are defined as census tracts with at least three of four characteristics.

Social Policy

Government policies have encouraged suburban sprawl and contributed to the problems of rural areas and inner cities. Revitalized areas show that centrally located properties are still valuable. During the 1980s, the federal government reduced spending on housing assistance. In the late 1980s and early 1990s, local government began setting up funds to provide housing. The Bush administration's efforts to increase domestic security and fight terrorism combined with tax cuts will increase deficits. This may compound the problems associated with homelessness.

A survey conducted in 2001 by the U.S. Conference of Mayors found significant increases in homelessness and in the demand for emergency food supplies in twenty-seven American cities. Only one-third of the cities surveyed reported they had enough food to feed their hungry populations adequately. While both conservatives and liberals recognize society's need to address the plight of inner-city communities, the strategy of creating empowerment zones to attract new businesses has yet to prove its worth.

Going Beyond Left and Right

Dislike of city life seems fairly evenly split among those on the left and the right. People who can leave often abandon inner-city neighborhoods. Empowerment zones are popular with both among conservative and liberal policy makers.

RESEARCH NAVIGATOR EXERCISES

ContentSelect

Use the sociology database and enter the keyword *cities*. Look for articles that describe or investigate cities and the sociological phenomena that accompany urban centers. One phenomenon is *institutional racism.* Read Juan Carlos Gonzalez's article, "The Ordinary-Ness of Institutional Racism" (*AN 26069487*) (Fall, 2007), which describes the history of segregation of Latinos(as) in our nation's school systems. Ask yourself whether many phenomena discussed in this chapter are, in fact, more "ordinary" than meets the eye. That is, the problems experienced by our nation's cities are, indeed, commonplace and perhaps even predictable in view of how our society is configured. Do you agree with Gonzalez's assessment? Why or why not?

New York Times Online

Use sociology as the subject, and enter the keyword *homelessness*. Read the article by Randal Archibold, "Los Angeles to Permit Sleeping on Sidewalks" (10/11/07). Imagine yourself as a resident of a large city like Los Angeles. Would you be in favor of allowing homeless people to sleep on public sidewalks? Why or why not?

Link Library

Use sociology as the subject and then click on H for homelessness. Look for the link to the U.S. Department of Housing and Urban Development's (HUD) page on homelessness. This page links to many valuable resources on homelessness. On this page, look for the topic, New Federal Response to Homelessness, and click on "find out more...". You will then go to a lengthy list of articles that describe the Bush administration's plan to attack the problem of homelessness. Return to the HUD page on homelessness and look at the other resources. For example, click on the National Alliance to End Homelessness link and read about their efforts to end homelessness.

PRACTICE TEST

MULTIPLE CHOICE QUESTIONS: Select the one best answer for each question below.

1. ______ is a way of life that depends on industry, mass communication, a mobile population, and mass consumer markets.
   a. Urbanism
   b. Industrialism
   c. Communitarianism
   d. none of the above

2. According to the text, by the year ______, most people will live in cities.
   a. 2010
   b. 2025
   c. 2050
   d. 2075

3. Adequate water supply and waste disposal systems were developed in the U.S. by the __________ century.
   a. seventeenth
   b. eighteenth
   c. nineteenth
   d. twentieth

4. Which of the following groups have experienced high rates of segregation throughout the nation's history?
   a. African Americans
   b. Asians
   c. Italians
   d. Poles

5. Wirth's theory of urbanization claims that cities
   a. create unique subcultures.
   b. increase social and personality disorders.
   c. increase personal freedoms and autonomy.
   d. none of the above

6. Herbert Gans's classic study *The Urban Villagers* focused on which ethic group?
   a. Muslim
   b. African American
   c. Italian
   d. Polish

7. _______ theorists see the city as a mosaic of social worlds—intimate social circles with their roots in kinship, ethnicity, neighborhoods, and life styles.
   a. Critical
   b. Subcultural
   c. Organic
   d. Compositional

8. Critical Urban theory argues that
   a. cities are a mosaic of social worlds.
   b. cities produce major social psychological changes in people.
   c. community ties are enhanced in the inner city.
   d. businesses in search of profits have contributed to urban sprawl.

9. Which of the following is considered to be larger?
   a. urban centers
   b. PMSA
   c. CMSAs
   d. ZPGs

10. Although they are not growing rapidly, metropolitan regions in the _____ remain the largest on the continent.
   a. Northwest
   b. Northeast
   c. Southeast
   d. Southern California

11. Edge cities are
   a. suburban developments with malls and gated housing.
   b. large urban clusters that attract business and shopping, but little else.
   c. rural cities.
   d. inner cities that are financially doomed.

12. Which of the following is NOT a consequence of surburbanization?
   a. the loss of industry to nearby suburbs along the highways
   b. increased funds for inner-city renovations
   c. the concentration of public housing in cities
   d. the tendency for homeowners to be concentrated outside cities in suburbs

13. High-tech industries prefer to locate near
   a. major universities.
   b. railroads.
   c. interstates.
   d. inner cities.

14. ______ refers to the flight to the suburbs of middle- and upper-middle-class families.
   a. Regeneration
   b. Suburbanization
   c. Deurbanization
   d. Decentralization

15. Of every $100.00 spent by the federal government, how much goes toward transportation?
   a. $2.00
   b. $8.00
   c. $10.00
   d. $14.00

16. A trend that has contributed to the urban housing problem is ______, or the return of affluent, single people and childless couples to selected central-city neighborhoods.
   a. reurbanization
   b. gentrification
   c. citification
   d. downtowning

17. According to Martha Burt of the Urban Institute, on any given day, at least ______ people are homeless in the United States.
   a. 800,000
   b. 200,000
   c. 500,000
   d. 1,500,000

18. The Census Bureau divides urban regions into ______, areas that are relatively homogeneous in population, socioeconomic status, and living conditions.
   a. census areas
   b. statistical areas
   c. cosmopolitan areas
   d. census tracts

19. Which of the following is NOT a result of urban renewal projects?
   a. facilitation of gentrification
   b. removal of slum housing
   c. settlement of original residents into redevelopments
   d. restriction of federal public housing to the very poor

20. Neighborhood distress is measured in terms of which variables?
   a. poverty
   b. joblessness
   c. teenage school dropouts
   d. all of the above

ESSAY QUESTIONS

1. Describe the urbanizing world; be sure to explain what is needed to urbanize and to identify some of the problems associated with this process.

2. Describe the American city; be sure to discuss antiurban bias, the composition of urban populations, and voluntary/involuntary segregation.

3. Compare and contrast the major theories of urbanization.

4. Define each of the following: CMSA, MSA, and PMSA.

5. Describe and discuss the transportation boom.

ANSWERS TO MULTIPLE CHOICE QUESTIONS

1.	a	11.	b
2.	a	12.	b
3.	d	13.	c
4.	a	14.	d
5.	b	15.	a
6.	c	16.	b
7.	c	17.	a
8.	d	18.	d
9.	c	19.	c
10.	b	20.	d

CHAPTER FOURTEEN

Population and Immigration

CHAPTER OUTLINE

- I. The World's Population
    - A. Measures of Population Growth
        - 1. Population Decline and World Migrations
    - B. The Demographic Transition
    - C. Rising Expectations
        - 1. Energy Consumption and Quality of Life
    - D. Food and Hunger
        - 1. Starvation in the Midst of Plenty
- II. Population Control
    - A. Family Planning
    - B. Zero Population Growth (ZPG)
    - C. Population Control in LDCs
- III. The U.S. Population
- IV. Immigration and Its Consequences
    - A. Immigration to the United States: A Brief History
        - 1. The Early Colonial Period (to 1790)
        - 2. Old Northwest European Migration (1820-1885)
        - 3. The Intermediate Migration from Southern and Eastern Europe (1885-1940)
        - 4. The Post-World War II Refugee Period (to 1968)
        - 5. The New Immigration (1968-Present)
        - 6. Once Again a Nation of Immigrants
    - B. Recent Trends in Immigration to the United States
    - C. Urban Concentration of Immigrants
    - D. Undocumented Immigrants
        - 1. Modes of Entry to the United States
- V. Social Policy
    - A. Immigration Reform?
    - B. Future Prospects
- VI. Going Beyond Left and Right
- VII. Summary
- VIII. Key Terms
- IX. Social Problems Online
- X. Research Navigator

LEARNING OBJECTIVES

After reading Chapter Fourteen you should:

1. Be aware of the way in which the world's population has grown, especially in the last two or three centuries.
2. Be familiar with the different measures of population growth.

3. Know what is meant by the concept of "demographic transition."
4. Understand the concept of "rising expectations."
5. Understand the relationship between amount of food and access to food.
6. Be familiar with strategies to control population growth, including family planning and Zero Population Growth, and population control in less developed nations.
7. Know about population growth in the United States, and which areas have experienced the greatest growth.
8. Be familiar with the various waves of immigration to the United States, from the early Colonial period to the present.
9. Be familiar with recent trends in immigration.
10. Know about the concentration of immigrants in key urban areas, and know what is meant by "chain migration."
11. Be familiar with the situation concerning undocumented immigrants.
12. Understand the social policy implications of recent immigration legislation and how the political climate affects immigration issues.

KEY TERMS

crude birthrate
rate of population growth (natural increase)
demographic transition
standard of living
level of living
chain migration
political refugee
overstayer
family reconciliation

CHAPTER SUMMARY

The World's Population

The average population growth rate before 1650 is thought to have been about two thousandths of a percent per year; in 1650, the population is estimated to have been 500 million. By 1900, the rate had increased to a half of 1 percent, and by 1960, it was 2 percent. By 1950, the world's population reached 2.5 billion; in 1999, it was 6 billion. While not likely, if the population continues to grow at this rate, it would double in about 45 years.

The ***crude birthrate*** refers to the number of births per 1,000 population. The ***rate of population growth (natural increase)*** refers to the difference between the crude birthrate and the death rate: usually, it is expressed as a percentage. Population can also be affected by migration to and from the unit.

People are not reproducing at a higher rate, but more people are living to the age of fertility. Most nations have a growth rate between .1 to 3.0 percent; 2 percent or more is "explosive." For less developed nations, growth rates of 1 percent are unlikely to occur in the near future. Russia, however, is an unusual case of population decline.

The ***demographic transition*** is a process that entails a shift from high birth and death rates to high birth and lower death rates to lower birth and lower death rates. The first stage is characteristic of peasant and primitive populations; the last is characteristic of industrialized populations. This process first occurred in northwestern Europe, and has taken place wherever industrial technology has taken hold. This includes Europe, North America, Australia, New Zealand, Japan, Singapore, Taiwan, and Hong Kong. Large areas of Asia, Africa, and Latin American are in the middle phase.

The United States is attractive to immigrants from Mexico, Haiti, the Dominican Republic, and Puerto Rico because those countries experience the stresses of overpopulation, while the United States has a slow rate of population growth. According to demographer Samuel Preston, low population growth in the non-European industrialized nations is due to several factors, including use of contraception, abortion, a reduction in family size desires, and a decline in the proportion of the population who are married. Preston identifies a decline or delay in the proportion who are married as the most significant of these.

Improved living conditions in some LDCs has led to a state of mind known as *rising expectations*, in which people anticipate more widespread improvements. The ***standard of living*** is what people want or expect in the way of material well-being. The ***level of living*** is what people actually get. In many less developed nations, there is a gap between these, and this produces frustration and political instability.

Literacy rates have improved for many countries; women especially have made significant progress in literacy. Energy consumption is one measure of quality of life. By this measure, stark disparities exist. The United States uses about 343 million BTUs of energy per person per year. The rates for other countries are France, 186; the U.K., 167; Mexico, 63; Columbia, 28; India, 15.

Almost three-quarters of a billion people are hungry in a world where there is plenty to eat. Every 3.6 seconds someone somewhere dies of hunger. Children account for 75 percent of these deaths. Food is actually plentiful in the world today. However, almost 15 percent of the world's population eats less than 2,000 calories per day. This population is chronically undernourished and experiences lowered resistance to disease. While food supplies have been increasing and cost of food decreasing, political unrest and corruption prevent food aid from reaching target populations. Wages have declined in many areas, making for many hardships. In contrast, in Western Europe and North America, the average person's diet supplies about 3,500 calories per day. One of the paradoxes of world hunger is that food supplies have been increasing over the past twenty years while the cost of food has been decreasing.

Population Control

Efforts to control population can take any of three basic approaches: reduce the growth rate, control the fertility rate to achieve zero population growth, or achieve a negative rate of growth. All these involve reduction of the birthrate. Voluntary efforts to limit births usually take the form of family planning. In the United States, Margaret Sanger played an important role in family planning. She opened the first birth control clinic in the United States in 1916; by 1965, roughly 85 percent of all married women used some form of birth control. By 2004, 98 percent of women who had ever been sexually active used at least one contraceptive method.

The organization Zero Population Growth (ZPG) promotes ending population growth through lowered birth rates by educating the public and taking political action. ZPG has encountered some opposition on social and economic grounds; zero population growth would change the age composition of the population and could reduce growth in the economy. Family planning and population control are non-synonymous.

Some countries (e.g., India) have used compulsory methods like sterilization. Population growth has slowed in Brazil, so that it is now similar to European industrialized nations. Reasons for the decline are diverse, but include a desire to limit births; this desire probably stems from increased education of women and the influence of the mass media.

The U.S. Population

The U.S. population growth is about 1 percent per year. This is due to more births than deaths and net migration. Assuming rates of immigration remain high, the U.S. population will continue to increase while those of other developed nations will slowly decrease. The Sunbelt and the western states have experienced rapid growth. Age and income disparities between old and new ethnic groups have increased.

Immigration and Its Consequences

The United States leads the world in the total number of immigrants. It is often said that the United States is a nation of immigrants; this diversity of people is one of the most important aspects of American culture. Immigration has also led to the exclusion of Native Americans, ethnic/racial conflict, competition, illegal immigration, exploitation of illegal aliens, and stress associated with caring for newcomers.

In the early colonial period (to 1790), the major population groups other than Native Americans had come from Great Britain and accounted for 77 percent of the total population. African and native-born slaves of African origin accounted for 19 percent, German immigrants 4 percent, Irish 3 percent, and Dutch 2 percent.

Between 1820-1885, the largest groups came from northern and western Europe, especially Germany, Ireland, and England. The Chinese were the most significant nonwhite immigrant group during this period. Between 1885-1940, the major immigrant groups were Italian, Poles, Hungarians, Serbians, Croatians, Greeks, and Jews. Nativism led to the Oriental exclusion movement. During this period, Congress passed the Immigration Act of 1921, which limited immigration to 150,000 per year. Before 1921, there had been no specific limits on immigration. After WWII, many Europeans had lost their homes, so in 1945, Congress agreed to admit 185,000 immigrants per year.

In 1968 and 1980, Congress increased immigration quotas. Priority is given to political or religious refugees or those who have close relatives living in the United States.

In the past few years the United States has been turning once again into a nation of immigrants.

Recent Trends in Immigration to the United States

By 2000, liberalized immigration laws made the United States among the world-leading immigrant-receiving populations. Slightly more than 10 percent of the population is foreign born. Although the immigrants themselves are not a problem, anti-immigrant feelings create hostility and tension. Illegal immigration is a severe social problem.

Most immigrants to the United States remain in only a few cities and regions (New York, Los Angeles, Miami, and Chicago are preferred destinations). Concentrations of immigrants in urban areas create non-English-speaking enclaves where education becomes a problem. ***Chain migration*** refers to the tendency of immigrants to migrate to areas where they have kin. The uneven distribution of immigrants adds to the cost of education and health care. Recent immigrants may experience hostility and competition; children and adolescents may form defensive gangs. However, some groups, especially Chinese and Koreans, may impose high achievement standards.

No one knows for sure how many undocumented immigrants there really are in the U.S. Every year, the United States Immigration and Naturalization Service finds more than 1.2 million illegal immigrants, many of whom are deported. Undocumented workers are easily exploited by others and may become "enslaved" to pay off debts to the smuggling ring; others work for low wages. Illegal residents may help some industries to survive, however.

Nearly half of all undocumented immigrants arrive legally as visitors to the United States, but they become ***overstayers***, and consequently illegal, when they exceed the time allocated to them to visit or reside in the United States. As much as 45 percent of the unauthorized immigrant population falls into this category of overstayers.

Social Policy

Terrorist attacks and the threat of war in the Middle East have created problems for immigrants. There are proponents and opponents of immigration; the former see it as a good thing while the latter believe it creates job competition and reduced wages. Republicans and Democrats have come into conflict over population policy. Republicans want to restrict programs to control population growth, while Democrats favor such programs.

The International Conference on Population and Development, held in Cairo in 1994, addressed population policies and the role of women in regulating fertility choices. In the United States, population policies focus mainly on immigration, especially illegal immigration. In 1986, Congress passed the Immigration Reform and Control Act, which makes employers subject to civil penalties for each illegal immigrant they hire. It also offered legal status to illegal aliens who entered the United States before January 1, 1982. Welfare reform hits legal immigrants hard because 1996 welfare reform laws deny benefits to legal immigrants who are not citizens. Social scientific research plays an important part in the debate about immigration policies.

It is very likely that the next Congress, to be elected along with a new president in 2008, will be able to pass an immigration bill with many of the features of the one that was defeated in 2007. The defeated bill would have placed far greater emphasis on the skills of individuals who seek to immigrate to the United States than on whether they have family members already in the country (the latter policy is known as ***family reconciliation***).

Going Beyond Left and Right

There are no clear left and right views on immigration. Some conservatives recognize the need for low-wage workers; others are concerned about the impact on welfare rolls. Some liberals see immigration as part of the American democratic tradition, while others are concerned that immigrants may drive down wages.

RESEARCH NAVIGATOR EXERCISES

ContentSelect

Select sociology as the database and use *illegal immigration* as the keywords. Read "Mexico's Hand in Illegal Immigration" (*AN 25455456*) (6/20/07). There are many recently published articles that identify Mexico as the major problem with illegal immigration to the U.S.. Do you agree? Why or why not? Do you think more stringent border patrol is the answer? What suggestions do you have?

New York Times Online

Select sociology as the subject and enter the keywords *family planning*. Read Elisabeth Rosenthal's article, "Legal or Not, Abortion Rates Compare" (10/12/07). Write a short summary of Rosenthal's principal conclusions. What is the significance of her findings for world population? Does what you have read change any of your previous views about abortion and family planning?

Link Library

Select sociology as the subject, and click on I for infant mortality. Next, click on the Statistical Rolodex to look at the data the Centers for Disease Control maintains on infant mortality. Why do you think that the United States has one of the higher rates of infant mortality? What might be done to reduce this rate? Use the back key to return to the Link Library links page on infant mortality, and click on Statistical Data Worldwide. This will take you to UNICEF's page on statistical data. Click on each of the following topics: water, sanitation, and guinea worm. For each of these topics, list all the factors that must be addressed to deal with each problem.

PRACTICE TEST

MULTIPLE CHOICE QUESTIONS: Select the one best answer for each of the following questions.

1. A common measure of population growth is the _____________
   a. crude birthrate.
   b. murder rate.
   c. abortion rate.
   d. degree of urbanization.

2. If the population in developing countries were to continue to grow at the current rate, the population in these nations would double by ___________.
   a. 2025
   b. 2050
   c. 2075
   d. 3000

3. The first stage of the demographic transition consists of a
   a. low birthrate; low death rate.
   b. low birthrate; high death rate.
   c. high birthrate; low death rate.
   d. high birth rate; high death rate.

4. Demographic transitions are
   a. complete in all nations.
   b. in their third stage in industrialized nations.
   c. absent in developing nations.
   d. no longer a factor in population changes.

5. The demographic transition started in
   a. northwestern Europe.
   b. East Asia.
   c. Latin America.
   d. none of the above

6. Which of the following countries remains in the second stage of the demographic transition?
   a. New Zealand
   b. Singapore
   c. Sweden
   d. Mexico

7. Currently, the United States admits about ____ immigrants annually.
   a, 1,200,000
   b. 1,600,000
   c. 800,000
   d. 200,000

8. The illiteracy rate in Egypt is 49.2 percent. What is the rate in Cuba?
   a. less than 5 percent
   b. about 50 percent
   c. 90 percent
   d. 98 percent

9. According to the text, which of the following are true with respect to food and hunger in the world?
   a. While malnourishment is a problem, starvation is not.
   b. There is simply not enough food to feed everyone.
   c. The cost of food has risen dramatically, so the poor simply cannot afford it.
   d. The cost of food has been decreasing, but the wages of the poor have fallen.

10. Amartya Sen's Law says the shortfalls in food supply do not cause widespread deaths in a democracy because vote-seeking politicians will undertake relief efforts; but even modest food shortfalls can create deadly famines in ____ societies.
   a. tribal
   b. totalitarian
   c. communist
   d. welfare state

11. _________opened the first birth control clinic and was jailed for doing so.
   a. Margaret Sanger
   b. Florence Nightingale
   c. Mother Theresa
   d. Betty Friedan

12. Which of the following has reduced the fertility rate in Brazil?
   a. a one child policy
   b. mandatory sterilization for women with more than three children
   c. legalized abortion
   d. birth control pills and aspirations for consumer goods

13. Which of the following countries will most likely experience an increase in population by 2050?
   a. the United States
   b. Russia
   c. Japan
   d. Germany

14. During the period of the northwestern European migration, the most significant nonwhite immigrant group was the
   a. Japanese.
   b. Chinese.
   c. Koreans.
   d. Vietnamese.

15. Current immigration policy in the United States gives priority to immigrants who
   a. are political refugees.
   b. are religious refugees.
   c. had close relatives living in the U.S.
   d. all of the above

16. The phenomenon of ____ migration, the primary cause of the urban concentration of immigrants to the United States, refers to the tendency of immigrants to migrate to areas where they have kin and others from their home communities.
a. kinship
b. funnel
c. chain
d, holistic

17. Worldwide, there are approximately ______ refuges.
a. 2,000,000
b. 8,000,000
c. 15,000,000
d. 20,000,000

18. Illegal immigrants who have exceeded the amount of time allocated to them to visit or reside in the United States are known as
a. interlopers.
b. overstayers.
c. invaders.
d. aliens.

19. In the United States, population-related policies focus primarily on
a. contraception.
b. abortion.
c. zero population growth.
d. immigration.

20. __________ is a policy that emphasizes whether a potential immigrant has family members already in the country.
a. Family reconciliation
b. Skill recognition
c. Family needs
d. Domestic partnership

ESSAY QUESTIONS

1. Discuss the difference between "standard of living" and "level of living." How do they relate to the issue of rising expectations?

2. Discuss the various methods of population control in less developed countries. What are some of the social consequences of these practices?

3. Discuss the history of immigration to the United States. What are some of the recent trends?

4. Describe the problem of urban concentration of immigrants in the United States. What are some of the consequences of this pattern for both the immigrants and the larger society?

5. Describe the role of politics in social policy debates on the topic of immigration. Be sure to note the impact of various pieces of legislation on immigration.

ANSWERS TO MULTIPLE CHOICE QUESTIONS

1.	a	11.	a
2.	b	12.	d
3.	d	13.	a
4.	b	14.	b
5.	a	15.	d
6.	d	16.	c
7.	c	17.	d
8.	a	18.	b
9.	d	19.	d
10.	b	20.	a

CHAPTER FIFTEEN

Technology and the Environment

CHAPTER OUTLINE

I. The Nature of Technology
  A. Technological Dualism
  B. Technology and Global Inequality
  C. The Digital Divide
II. Controlling Technology
  A. Autonomous Technology
  B. Automation
  C. Whistle-Blowers
  D. Identity Theft—A Global Crime Wave in Cyberspace
  E. Bureaucracy and Morality
III. Technology and Institutions
    1. Transhumanism
IV. Technology and the Natural Environment
V. Environmental Stress
  A. Origins of the Problem
  B. Air Pollution
    1. Effects on Human Health
    2. Economic Effects
    3. Ecological Effects
    4. The Global-Warming Controversy
    5. Radioactivity
  C. Water Pollution
  D. Solid-Waste Disposal
    1. Environmental Racism, Environmental Justice
    2. Toxic Wastes
    3. Radioactive Wastes
  E. Other Hazards
    1. Land Degradation
    2. Noise Pollution
    3. Chemical Contamination and Globalization of the Food Supply
    4. Large-Scale Engineering Projects
VI. The United States and the World Environment
VII. Social Policy
  A. Policy on Global Warming
    1. Pollution Credits
    2. Science and Policy Making
  B. Appropriate Technology
  C. Future Prospects
VIII. Going Beyond Left and Right
IX. Summary
X. Key Terms
XI. Social Problems Online
XII. Research Navigator

LEARNING OBJECTIVES

After reading Chapter Fifteen you should:

1. Be able to define technology.
2. Understand what is meant by the digital divide and technological dualism.
3. Know how social scientists look at autonomous technology.
4. Be able to discuss the impact of automation on society and the economy.
5. Understand the challenges faced by whistle-blowers.
6. Understand technology and bureaucracies and the impact on morality.
7. Know what is meant by cultural lag.
8. Be able to distinguish environmental stress from environmental pollution.
9. Know the impact of pollution on human health, the economy, and the ecology.
10. Know what global warming is and some of its suggested causes.
11. Be able to list some of the other environmental hazards and their impacts.
12. Be aware of changes in environmental social policy over the past few decades.

KEY TERMS

technology
technological dualism
digital divide
whistle-blowers
cultural lag
cyborg
environmental stress
environmental pollution
acid rain
global warming
appropriate technology

CHAPTER SUMMARY

The Nature of Technology

Technology is the combination of all methods for increasing the productivity of labor and capital. Methods are the apparatus, activities, and organization associated with technology. Some technology is revolutionary, but some involves smaller innovations that spur minor adjustments in other sectors of society or among small numbers of people.

The term ***technological dualism*** refers to the fact that advances in technology can have both positive and negative impacts. Technological dualism can be seen in the types of jobs available. On the one hand, technology increases automation and creates new kinds of jobs. On the other hand, it displaces workers who become unemployed and must be retrained if they are to find employment.

The Human Development Report of the United Nations Development Programme concludes that there is a widening gap between the haves and the have-nots, between the knows and the know-nots due to unequal access to technology. The ***digital divide*** refers to the gap between those who have access to computers and the Internet and those who do not. In the United States the digital divide is closing, but it is still immense in the Third World.

Controlling Technology

Some people argue that technology is not controllable through democratic political institutions, while others argue that society adapts. Social scientists have argued that technology is not autonomous, but that we have created a web of dependency on technology that creates a technologic order. As a whole, the technological order supplies the basic necessities of life, along with innumerable extras. In the process, much of the life of society has been diverted from meeting the needs of survival to meeting the requirements of technology.

Automation increases the productivity of the economy, since a constant or decreasing number of workers can turn out more of a desired product. The question remains of whether the new wealth generated by higher productivity will be used to benefit the entire society or only individuals who are already wealthy. Evidence suggests that the contemporary effects of automation as measured by increasing productivity have been much less than the stereotypical image of robots that replace workers would suggest.

So many of the proposed solutions to technological problems are themselves new technologies that opportunities abound for abuse and personal profit through their application. People who see abuses of new technological systems often run grave personal risks when they attempt to expose them. These individuals are known as ***whistle-blowers***. The challenges faced by whistle-blowers are exemplified in the attempts to reveal design flaws in nuclear power plants and in known problems with the space shuttle Challenger.

Identity theft refers to the illegal possession of another person's private account numbers and the use of those numbers for fraudulent purposes. Recent estimates indicate that one in four American adults has been affected by identity theft and the overall value of losses is over $4 billion.

Today much of the productive activity that occurs in complex societies takes place in large bureaucratic organizations. With their orientation toward specified goals, their division of labor into narrowly defined roles, and their hierarchical authority structures, such organizations are supremely efficient. But some of the qualities of large organizations that make them so productive and valuable can also cause harm. For example, individuals may commit immoral acts because they are not personally responsible for those acts. Stanley Milgram was able to demonstrate this in a laboratory by inducing individuals to ostensibly apply electric shock to others by creating situations where the individuals did not feel responsible.

Technology and Institutions

Sociologists who study technology and the effects of technological change concern themselves with the relationships between technology and social institutions. ***Cultural lag*** theory suggests that two correlated parts of a culture can change at different rates. For example, social-welfare legislation lagged behind the change to an industrial society. Towns based on a single technology have suffered because the technology became obsolete. Sometimes the culture changes before the technology. For example, American dependence on the automobile has created a need for alternatives to fossil fuel before the technology has developed to meet that need. Sometimes this need for technology to catch up to the culture has created pressure to falsify data. Cases of announcements of cold fusion breakthroughs are instances of this.

Transhumanism is the very small but growing social movement that advocates the ethical use of technologies to enhance human capabilities. Transhumanists are fascinated by the idea of the ***cyborg***, a creature that is part human and part technological systems.

Technology and the Natural Environment

According to Barry Commoner, human civilization has been changing and becoming more complex at an accelerating rate. As the ability of humans to exploit the resources of the earth has grown, so has the size of human populations. These two factors are causing pollution and depletion of the natural environment as never before.

Sometimes technologies that seem benign and that we take for granted as part of everyday life have unanticipated consequences. In many cases the technology exists to control environmental damage, but powerful interests do not wish to shoulder the cost of doing so. In other cases, the technology does not yet exist. Environmental stress can best be understood as the interaction of three systems: the natural environment, the technological system, and the social system.

Environmental Stress

Environmental stress refers to what society does to the environment. Environmental stress is not pollution, although pollution is a form of it. ***Environmental pollution*** is the presence of agents added to the environment by society in kinds and quantities potentially damaging to human welfare or to organisms other than people.

Four concepts are basic to understanding environmental stress: interdependence, diversity, limits, and complexity. Interdependence means that everything is related to and depends on everything else; diversity refers to the existence of many different life and life support forms; limits refers to the finite limit to growth of any organism and to the limit of a given species in an environment; complexity refers to the intricacy of the relationships that constitute the web.

Because of complexity, interventions in the environment frequently lead to unanticipated and undesired consequences. One of the major difficulties in dealing with environmental stress is the number of problems involved and the extent to which they are interrelated.

Human activities are overwhelming the atmosphere's ability to cleanse itself. Although air pollution varies by locality, there are some common components: hydrocarbons; oxides of carbon, nitrogen, and sulfur; lead and other metals; and particulate matter. In urban areas, almost half the air pollution comes from motor vehicles; the remainder from the burning of fossil fuels. Pollution is particularly severe in parts of the world where leaded gasoline is unregulated and large populations still burn firewood.

Research shows that continued exposure to air pollutants increases incidences of such illnesses as bronchitis, emphysema, and lung cancer. Economic effects include maintenance and cleaning cost; costs associated with lower crop production; and increased medical care costs.

Air pollution may have a dangerous long-term effect on the earth's ecosystem. Fluorocarbon gasses are depleting the ozone layer, which increases skin cancer and crop failure rates. Air pollution also causes acid rain, which is rainfall that contains large concentrations of sulfur dioxide. ***Acid rain*** has a highly detrimental effect on forests and lakes, causing severe damage to trees, fish, and other forms of aquatic life as well as polluting water supplies.

Pollution could be causing an increase in global temperature. There has been an increase in global temperature since the industrial revolution and the rate of increase is growing. At present, there is widespread consensus that ***global warming*** is real, but there is continued debate about the basic causes of the trend and its implications.

In 1986, explosions at the nuclear power plant in Chernobyl in the former Soviet Union released a cloud of radioactive gases over central and northern Europe. Many environmental scientists fear that the health of people in the former Soviet Union and Europe could be severely affected for decades. Radioactivity is a severe form of air pollution that increases the probability that people will die from cancer.

Just like air can cleanse itself if not overburdened, so, too, can rivers, lakes, and oceans. But we have been discharging waste, directly or indirectly, into our waterways in amounts that prohibit natural purification. Current farming practices, such as extensive use of nitrate and phosphate fertilizers, seriously impair water quality. Long-lasting pesticides and radioactive substances are especially dangerous because they accumulate in the tissues of animals that eat them. This is a serious problem because such substances become more concentrated as it ascends the food chain. Another form of water pollution is thermal pollution. The effluents of many factories and generating plants are warming waterways, which can be ecologically devastating.

Americans had 410 million tons of solid waste in 2005. There are two primary ways of disposing of solid waste: landfills and incineration. Although landfills are supposed to meet certain sanitary standards, violations are common. Improperly designed municipal incinerators are major contributors to urban air pollution. The large-scale introduction of plastics and other synthetics has produced a new waste disposal problem since they remain in their original state when they are buried or dumped. If they are burned, they become air pollutants.

Solid waste dumpsites are often located near low-income neighborhoods on the outskirts of metropolitan regions or in rural areas, which are frequently populated by minorities. Many local activists and residents of these neighborhoods term such dumping *environmental racism.* Consequently, there are higher rates of illness because of contaminated runoff from these sites. Another problem is toxic wastes or residues from the production of plastics, pesticides, and other products. These have typically been buried. The famous case of Love Canal demonstrates the impact this can have.

Spent fuel from nuclear power plants must be deposited in extremely well-protected conditions because it remains dangerous for up to 1,000 years. Additionally, there are dangers associated with transporting radioactive material to dump sites. Other threats arise from the indiscriminate use of technological knowledge. These include land degradation, noise pollution, chemical hazards, and the undesirable consequences of certain large-scale engineering projects.

Through greed and/or ignorance of ecological principles, we have diminished or destroyed the capacity of large land areas to support life. We are only beginning to recognize the possible consequences. By 2000, an estimated 36 percent of the earth's land area was threatened with desertification. Hearing loss caused by excessive noise now affects about 10 million people in the United States. There is evidence that noise pollution can adversely affect reading scores of school children.

There has been a proliferation of chemicals used in food production. Little is known about the long-term effects of continual ingestion of these substances. Large dams and strip mining can have tremendous environmental effects.

The United States and the World Environment

Because Americans are among the wealthiest, the most educated, and the most polluting of the earth's peoples, environmental scientists often argue that they bear a large share of the responsibility for wise management of the planet. Americans eat more food, but the food they eat includes a much larger proportion of meat than grain. The grain used in meat production for Americans could nourish hungry people elsewhere in the world. The United States consumes 25 percent of the world's fossil fuel and produces 72 percent of its hazardous waste.

The significance of these facts is twofold: First, the industrialized nations consume a disproportionate share of the total food and energy resources, leaving comparatively little for the majority of the world's population. Second, the United States contributes to environmental problems both at home and abroad.

Social Policy

One of the Bush administration's most controversial environmental rulings was refusing to sign the international treaty known as the Kyoto Protocol.

In 2002, the Bush administration announced a policy of funding additional studies of global warming, which was denounced by environmental groups in the United States and throughout the world because these groups argue that immediate actions are necessary. Australia and the United States are the two major nations that refused to sign the Kyoto accords.

The creation of markets to buy and sell pollution credits is a more conservative antipollution policy favored by the Bush administration and by many experts on global pollution problems.

There is ongoing conflict between the Bush administration and the nation's scientists who argue that something needs to be done right away about global warming. The Bush administration prefers to speak of global climate change rather than the more alarming term global warming.

Social policies that deal with technologies and their environmental consequences are extremely controversial especially when potentially lucrative products are involved and point up the significance of scientific assessment of the environmental impact of proposed technologies. Appropriate technologists advocate major changes in technology. In most cases ***appropriate technology*** is smaller-scale technology.

Facing intense pressure from nations that have taken the lead in addressing the problem of global warming, in 2007 the U.S. Congress began taking steps to establish the basic regulatory mechanisms necessary for a "cap and trade" approach to the reduction of greenhouse gasses.

RESEARCH NAVIGATOR

ContentSelect

Use the sociology database and enter the keyword *global warming*. Read Maya Grinberg's article, "That Sinking Feeling" (*AN 26019528*) (Aug, 2007). Grinberg charges that the world's cities are sinking because of global warming – especially those population centers that are located in coastal regions. What are your reactions to her article? Do you agree or disagree with her assessment? Why?

New York Times Online

Use the environmental studies database and enter the keyword *air pollution*. Read Elisabeth Rosenthal's article (10/13/07), "Award Underlines Danger of Climate Change." Rosenthal's article punctuates the significance of Al Gore having been identified as a co-recipient of the Nobel Peace Prize for his work on climate change and global warming. After you have read the article, compare your views of Mr. Gore as a politician versus a humanitarian.

Link Library

Use sociology as the subject. Click on E and then on environmental sociology. Then click on "Another definition." How is environmental sociology defined here? Next, return to the Link Library and click on P for pollution. Read about water, noise, air, and other types of environmental pollution in our environment on this page. Look also at the text of the Clean Air Acts. Next, return to the heading "water pollution," and click on it. You will be sent to the Environmental Protection Agency's Web page on water pollution. Click on "EPA home." You will be sent to the home page for the agency. Look for the key topics column, and click on "Cleanup." Next, select the "Superfund cleanup process." This will describe the Superfund program and what is involved in cleanup. Read about the Superfund program by clicking on "About Superfund" in the topics on the left side of the page; next, look at the right side of the page for "Tools." Click on the Enviromapper to locate Superfund sites in your state or community. Investigate the status of these sites. Were you surprised at the number of Superfund sites in the United States, in your state, in your community? Why or why not? What is the status of the cleanup in your state?

PRACTICE TEST

MULTIPLE CHOICE QUESTIONS: Select the one best answer for each of the following questions.

1. Which of the following is NOT one of Langdon Winner's dimensions for understanding the broader meaning of technology?
   a. intrinsic philosophy
   b. technological tools, instruments, machines, and gadgets
   c. technical skills, procedures, and routines
   d. the organization networks associated with activities and apparatus

2. The fact that advances in technology can have both positive and negative impacts is termed
   a. the latent technology effect.
   b. the technological split factor.
   c. technological dualism.
   d. the technology divide.

3. The gap between those with access to computers and the Internet and those without such access is referred to as the
   a. cybernetic rift.
   b. digital divide.
   c. technology crisis.
   d. Internet gap.

4. What was the name of the computer that ran the space mission in the film *2001: A Space Odyssey*?
   a. Jim
   b. Turk
   c. Lem
   d. Hal

5. People who see abuses of new technological systems and attempt to expose them are know as
   a. snitches.
   b. whistle-blowers.
   c. corporate tattle-tales.
   d. insiders.

6. In a hierarchical system, individuals may commit immoral acts because they
   a. do not feel personally responsible for them.
   b. don't care.
   c. have no morality.
   d. become sadistic.

7. According to William F. Ogburn, _____ takes place when one of two parts of culture which are correlated changes before or in greater degree than the other part does, thereby causing less adjustment between the two parts than existed previously.
   a. cold fusion
   b. anomie
   c. cultural lag
   d. social disintegration

8. A study of the impact of interstate highways on nonmetropolitan counties between 1950 and 1975 established an association between highway construction and
   a. air pollution.
   b. economic and population growth along the interstate corridor.
   c. global-warming.
   d. automotive technology innovations.

9. The cold fusion fiasco discussed in the text illustrates why
   a. the norms of science are valuable and need to be protected.
   b. cultural lag is unpredictable.
   c. environmental stress impairs scientific judgment.
   d. George W. Bush does not support Kyoto Protocol.

10. Environmental stress
   a. is the same as environmental pollution.
   b. includes concepts of interdependence, diversity, limits, and complexity.
   c. leads to burnout among scientists.
   d. has decreased since the 1950s.

11. In urban areas, almost _____ of the carbon monoxide in the air comes from motor vehicles.
   a. one-quarter
   b. one-half
   c. three-quarters
   d. none

12. ______ rain refers to rainfall that contains large concentrations of sulfur dioxide, which is emitted by utility and industrial plants in many parts of the nation.
   a. Acid
   b. Heavy
   c. Toxic
   d. Caustic

13. The Chernobyl accident
   a. created high levels of radioactive gases.
   b. was not reported for years after it occurred.
   c. had only short-term effects.
   d. highlighted the need for nuclear power.

14. Thermal pollution refers to
   a. pollution caused by mercury in thermometers.
   b. warmer water from effluents of factories and power plants.
   c. global warming.
   d. ozone depletion.

15. There is a growing tendency for solid-waste dumping to be a particular problem for African Americans and Latinos. This has been referred to as environmental
   a. discrimination.
   b. terrorism.
   c. prejudice.
   d. racism.

16. In 2005, the United States recycled about ____ percent of its solid waste.
   a. 10
   b. 20
   c. 30
   d. 50

17. Radioactive waste must be stored safely for up to _____ years before it becomes harmless.
   a. 100
   b. 500
   c. 1,000
   d. 5,000

18. The United States consumes ____ percent of the world's fossil fuels and produces 72 percent of its hazardous waste.
   a. 25
   b. 38
   c. 62
   d. 75

19. At present, there is widespread consensus among earth and environmental scientists that global warming is
   a. not caused by fluorocarbons.
   b. part of a natural cycle.
   c. a genuine threat.
   d. a mixed blessing.

20. Proponents of appropriate technology
   a. desire a return to preindustrial lifestyles.
   b. oppose large-scale technologies.
   c. are against the development of solar and wind energy.
   d. are opposed to government control of technology.

ESSAY QUESTIONS

1. Define technology and discuss the wider dimensions of it.
2. Discuss technological dualism; give examples.
3. Discuss how the social organization of technology could have an impact on morality.
4. Define cultural lag and give some examples.
5. Discuss the impact of automation on employment.
6. Distinguish environmental stress from environmental pollution.
7. Define and discuss environmental racism.
8. Why do some argue that the United States has more responsibility than other nations to do something about pollution?

ANSWERS TO MULTIPLE CHOICE QUESTIONS

1.	a	11.	b
2.	c	12.	a
3.	b	13.	a
4.	d	14.	b
5.	b	15.	d
6.	a	16.	c
7.	c	17.	c
8.	b	18.	a
9.	a	19.	c
10.	b	20.	b

CHAPTER SIXTEEN

War and Global Insecurity

CHAPTER OUTLINE

I. Terrorism, Global and Domestic
   A. Measuring Terrorism in the United States
      1. Patterns of Global Terrorism
   B. Origins of Terrorist Groups
   C. Terrorism and Religion
   D. Terrorism's Impact on Society
II. War and Its Effects
   A. Indirect Effects of War
   B. Effects of Nuclear War
   C. Rogue States and Weapons of Mass Destruction
III. Controlling Warfare
   A. War on Terrorists and the Rule of Law
   B. "Just Wars" and War Crimes
IV. Theories about War and Its Origins
   A. Ethological and Sociobiological Theories
   B. Clausewitz: War as State Policy
   C. Marx and Lenin on War
   D. Institutional and International Perspectives
      1. Institutional Forces within Nations
      2. The International Context of War and Peace
V. Social Policy
   A. Arms Control: A Promise Unfulfilled
   B. Dealing with Terrorism
   C. Future Prospects
VI. Going Beyond Left and Right
VII. Summary
VIII. Key Terms
IX. Social Problems Online
X. Research Navigator Exercises

LEARNING OBJECTIVES

After reading Chapter Sixteen you should:

1. Know the difference between war and terrorism.
2. Be able to define and discuss the different types of terrorism.
3. Be familiar with the origins of terrorism.
4. Be familiar with the indirect effects of war.
5. Understand the importance of military technology.

6. Identify some of the ways attempts have been made to control war.
7. Be able to discuss the theories of the causes of war and understand the ethological and sociobiological perspectives, the economic perspectives of Marx and Lenin, and political perspectives.

KEY TERMS

terrorism
narcoterrorism
state terrorism
revolutionary terrorism
nationalism

CHAPTER SUMMARY

Terrorism, Global and Domestic

The FBI defines ***terrorism*** as the unlawful use of force or violence against persons or property to intimidate or coerce a government, the civilian population, or any segment thereof, in furtherance of political or social objectives. ***Narcoterrorism*** is revenge on authorities to intimidate them into lax enforcement of laws. Terrorism of governments against their own people is repressive terrorism or ***state terrorism***. ***Revolutionary terrorism*** is the most common and often leads to the other types.

Terrorism is difficult to track because it is not always clear that people or groups seeking to further political aims perpetrate acts of violence. Also, groups that advocate violence may not be responsible for violence committed in their names. The American Terrorism Study, conducted by the FBI, studied domestic terrorism from 1980 to 1988. Groups studied espoused a wide range of ideologies, including Marxist, environmental, racist-white-supremacist, fundamentalist-antiabortionist, and extreme fascist. There were three times as many right wing groups as there were left wing groups. In a recent analysis of patterns of global terrorism, the Department of Homeland Security (2007) compiled and analyzed incidents of terrorism. Data from this study are summarized in **Table 16-1**.

Events in more troubled parts of the world lead to fluctuations in the number of terrorist acts. Peace in a region leads to fewer acts, worsening conditions lead to higher rates of terrorism.

In addition to its origins in political radicalism, terrorism may spring from various kinds of cults that have much in common despite differing ideologies. Agents of the state can perpetuate terrorism. Hitler and Stalin, for example, used brutality, fear, and legalized murder to subjugate the masses. Most terrorists are well educated from middle or upper classes. Leaders for al Qaeda, for example, were well educated from wealthy families. They seem to have been motivated by the failures at attempts to adopt Western ways. As individuals, terrorists want to save the world, although their concept of salvation is based on a limited set of inflexible beliefs. The terrorist believes that purity of motive justifies whatever methods are employed.

That so many terrorist individuals and groups are motivated by extreme religious beliefs and feelings is one of the chief ironies of the present war on terrorism. All major religions, including Christianity, Judaism, and Islam all have virulent strands. Like many fundamentalist belief systems, extreme forms of Islam tend to be totalitarian in that they seek to control the person's total life. They seek control through fear. In the process, a terrorist's victims become pawns in the struggle for social reform and are stripped of their human rights and identity. There are two types of victims: first, random victims, those who are in the wrong place at the wrong time and who are part of the terrorist's attempts to intimidate other members of the society; second, people who terrorists single out because of their prominence.

Terrorism can be extremely effective. The impact of terrorism in the United States includes increased fear and erosion of civil liberties as well as economic, health, and political consequences. It is too early, however, to assess the long-term impact the war on terrorism will have.

War and Its Effects

War is one of the most serious social problems one can imagine. Over the centuries warfare has taken millions of lives. The effects of war persist even after peace is declared. Soldiers are injured and require treatment after the war has ended. Some are disabled. The lower-class individuals are more likely to be put in dangerous military roles.

Not all war-related injuries are physical. War takes a psychological toll as well. Posttraumatic stress disorder is common among soldiers exposed to heavy combat. This is particularly true with Vietnam War veterans because it was a guerrilla war and resulted in more violence against civilians.

War often leads to mass migrations. This can occur as people look for new opportunities or to avoid danger. It can also occur because of government policies that force people to move. There are also indirect economic effects, such as lost productivity. Also war can impact the way people think, such as increased pessimism or disillusionment.

In the past 100 years, wars have become less frequent but more intense as military technology has become more lethal. Nuclear weapons can cause unimaginable destruction. The bomb on Hiroshima illustrates how destructive a nuclear bomb can be, even though it was tiny by today's standards. As the technologies of war have become more deadly, the ravages of war have become greater. Wars fought with swords and spears are less deadly than those fought after the invention of gunpowder. Armor, tanks, and bombs have increased the carnage. In 2001, the Natural Resource Defense Council reported that the 192 missile warheads on one U.S. Trident submarine – constituting less than 3 percent of the existing U.S. arsenal – could cause more than 50 million casualties if programmed to hit major urban areas of a nation.

Rogue states are nations whose governments refuse to adhere to the rule of law either on the domestic or the international stage, and routinely threaten their own citizens and those of other nations with violence and terror. North Korea, for example, has threatened to begin producing nuclear bombs. Other threats come from some former Soviet states, as well as other areas of instability, where extreme political instability and poverty create weak or nonexistent government controls. These areas are often the cradles of terrorism and areas where weapons of mass destruction could be circulated.

Improvements in military organization are also important to recognize. From the introduction of phalanx by the Greeks to modern military bureaucratization, military effectiveness has increased.

Controlling Warfare

Controversies over the possible use of torture in prisons run by American forces in Iraq, in Guantanamo, Cuba, and perhaps in other secret locations raise many questions about whether nations can protect their citizens from terrorist attacks without resorting to inhumane practices. In 2004, the Supreme Court rejected the U.S. government's attempts to detain an American citizen indefinitely without a trial.

There have also been improvements in controlling warfare as nations have developed complex rules on the rights and privileges of those who fight and that attempt to protect noncombatants. Underlying this body of law is the ancient concept of the "just war." There are two major branches of this doctrine: justification for going to war (*jus ad bellum*) and justifiable acts in wartime (*jus in bello*).

Theories about War and Its Origins

No single theory can fully explain any given war. Nevertheless, a number of theories have shed light on some of the forces that contribute to war. Ethologists and sociobiologists believe that a predisposition to aggression may have been transmitted genetically from one generation to the next. Konrad Lorenz concluded that aggression is an instinct in humans, as it is in lower animals. Sociobiologists point out that while humans inherit predispositions, behavior is also influenced by culture and can be controlled. Critics deny that genes influence human behavior in general and warfare in particular; instead they explain behavior in terms of learned responses.

In 1832, Carl von Clausewitz explained war in terms of the rational decisions of monarchs rather than irrational elements of human nature, like a predisposition for aggression. War is strictly a means to an end to be used only if its benefits outweigh its costs. Clausewitz took a simplistic view that the military functions to support the monarch, regardless of ambitions of the military. He also did not foresee the influence of the wealthy merchants and industrialists.

In the contemporary world, the social control of the armed forces remains a serous problem in many nations. In Latin America there has been a decline in the number of military dictatorships. Critics of American preparations for a second war with Iraq use Clausewitz's theory to argue that military power cannot operate effectively in a political vacuum or without the reinforcement of diplomacy.

Marx believed that political leaders acted as agents of the bourgeoisie in their struggle to improve business conditions and keep the proletariat under control. Lenin built on Marx and argued that war pitted the national ruling classes against one another; the workers had nothing to gain by taking up arms. Lenin contended that the violent overthrow of the bourgeoisie by the proletariat would eventually remove the motivation for warfare.

Marx and Lenin believed that economic interests shape most social phenomena, including warfare, but a number of social scientists have argued that noneconomic factors must be considered. There are two types of noneconomic explanations: institutional forces within nations and international factors.

Some social scientists have argued that keeping a large, well-equipped military force makes it easier for political leaders to choose war rather than negotiation as a tactic for handling international conflict. Others argue that a powerful military discourages other nations from starting wars.

C. Wright Mills suggested that during World War II the military gained influence with business out of necessity of winning the war. After the war, the influence remained and continues to shape American politics and economic development. Seymour Melman argues that managers at the top of the federal government have often made decisions that serve their own interests but damaged the economy and the interests of the rich. The Vietnam War, for example, resulted in high rates of inflation and diverted money that corporate executives could have invested for other purposes. The public is also an important consideration. As states have become more democratized, political leaders must consider the opinions of the public when making their decisions about war. In some cases, public opinions favor war, especially when ***nationalism***, or identification with the idea of nationhood and exaltation of the nation's culture and interests above those of all other states, is strong.

Because the supply of natural resources, power, prestige, and other valued commodities is limited, nations inevitably compete with one another. However, there are a number of forces that reduce incentives to wage war.

One such force is international cooperation. The League of Nations and later the United Nations are examples of international institutions designed to promote cooperation among nations. Research has shown that when the United States and other nations are drawn in as peacekeepers, such efforts are largely unsuccessful and the peacekeepers cannot leave.

International trade is another force that promotes peace. When influential citizens benefit economically from peaceful relations, support for war is diminished. Moreover, trade promotes a common outlook as well as common interests.

Social Policy

The United States has taken a "go it alone" attitude and refused to sign international accords on war crimes, nuclear proliferation, and biological weapons. This reinforces the belief that the United States is not exerting positive leadership in world peace.

The history of disarmament since nuclear weapons were invented consists of a series of limited agreements that have until very recently allowed the arms race to continue almost unabated. Despite their failure to ban nuclear weapons, the major powers have succeeded in formulating a number of treaties that limit certain weapons and regulate the spread of others.

The Strategic Arms Limitation Talks produced two agreements that are flawed in a number of ways. The Bush administration is developing an antimissile shield and has announced the United States reserves the right to take unilateral action in the Middle East and other areas. A serious problem created by smaller regional wars and arms sales to poor nations is the legacy they leave behind in the form of unexploded ammunition and buried land mines.

Terrorists use violence and drastic actions to attract media attention to their cause as well as to intimidate civilians and show governments that they can exert power. There are a number of policies that have proved effective against terrorism. An informed public that will cooperate with antiterrorist policies is extremely important in combating this social problem.

Going Beyond Left and Right

It is difficult to balance the power of government in the control of terrorism and individual rights. The right conditions need to be present for citizens to agree about what to do in order to make the U.S. safer from terrorism, and any consensus is not likely to last for very long.

RESEARCH NAVIGATOR EXERCISES

ContentSelect

Select the sociology database, and enter the keyword *terrorism*. Try to locate articles that explain the sources of terrorism, and also strategies for dealing with it. Try reading Maya Grinberg's article, "Mall Terror" (*AN 24884455*) (May, 2007). Everyone reading this will have shopped in a mall somewhere. After you have finished reading Grinberg's article, how comfortable do you think you will be the next time you are in a shopping mall? What do you think of Grinberg's assessment? What do you have to add?

New York Time Online

Use the sociology subject base, and enter the keyword *terrorism*. Read Heather Timmons and Eric Pfanner's article, "Europe Says It Will Unify Effort in Fight on Terrorism" (8/17/06). How does this article relate to the text's observations about global terrorism? Write a short summary of what you have learned from this article.

Link Library

Use sociology as the subject, and click on T for terrorism. Click on Document Archive. This website consists of partial data from the U.S. State Department's archives on patterns of terrorist attacks, 1993-1997. Click on each year, and count the number of incidences reported. Are you surprised at the number? Go back to the terrorism page, and scroll to the bottom of the list of websites and click on ICT. This is the website for the International Policy Institute for Terrorism and Counterterrorism. Click on International Terrorism on the left side of the page. Look at the Terror Attack Database. You can enter specific dates to get a detailed listing of attacks. Next, click on unconventional terrorism. Look at the types of unconventional terrorism and how they are defined. Which of these seems more likely and more dangerous to you? Why?

PRACTICE TEST

MULTIPLE CHOICE QUESTIONS: Select the one best answer for each of the following questions.

1. The terrorism of governments against their own people is called _____ terrorism.
   a. narco
   b. revolutionary
   c. state
   d. structural

2. The most common form of terrorism is
   a. narcoterrorism.
   b. state terrorism.
   c. revolutionary terrorism.
   d. none of the above

3. The terrorism of governments like that of Nigeria against their own people is known as __________ terrorism.
   a. revolutionary
   b. state
   c. narco
   d. structural

4. In March of 1997, thirty-nine members of a cult known as _______ were discovered in a mass suicide in an affluent San Diego suburb.
   a. the Branch Davidians
   b. the Ku Klux Klan
   c. the Moon Unification Church
   d. Heaven's Gate

5. Terrorist recruits are often
   a. poorly educated.
   b. from poverty stricken backgrounds.
   c. well educated.
   d. Islamic.

6. Which of the following is NOT an impact of terrorism?
   a. increasing fear of attack and heightened security
   b. erosion of civil liberties
   c. economic consequences
   d. none of the above

7. There are two types of victims of terrorism,
   a. random victims and prominent individuals.
   b. military and civilian casualties.
   c. males and females.
   d. direct and indirect casualties.

8. During World War II, 17 million soldiers were killed. How many civilians were killed?
   a. 1 million
   b. 11 million
   c. 23 million
   d. 35 million

9. Which period has been the deadliest in human history?
   a. the prehistoric period
   b. the middle ages
   c. the colonial period
   d. the twentieth century

10. In 2006, about ______ veterans were receiving compensation from the U.S. government for war-related disabilities.
   a. 500,000
   b. 1 million
   c. 2 million
   d. 5 million

11. One indirect effect of war is
   a. stimulation of the homeland economy.
   b. mass migration.
   c. increased civil liberties.
   d. decline in nationalism.

12. The first nuclear bomb used in war
   a. has not yet occurred.
   b. was dropped on Hiroshima in 1945.
   c. was used during the Vietnam War.
   d. was used during Desert Storm.

13. Nations whose governments refuse to adhere to the rule of law either on the domestic or the international stage, and routinely threaten their own citizens and those of other nations with violence and terror are called
   a. nation states.
   b. dictatorships.
   c. criminal states.
   d. rogue states.

14. Nuclear bombs ____ times more powerful than the one that fell on Hiroshima are now a standard part of the weapons systems of the major world powers
   a. 16
   b. 160
   c. 1,600
   d. 16,000

15. Which of the following is true with regard to *jus in bello*?
   a. The rules are difficult to enforce.
   b. The rules are frequently violated.
   c. Civilians are often killed.
   d. all of the above

16. Ethological theories of war rely on ______ explanations.
    a. cultural
    b. biological
    c. psychological
    d. political

17. __________ described war as an alternative to diplomacy, engaged in for the purposes of gaining land, prestige, and other benefits; strictly a means to an end.
    a. Carl von Clausewitz
    b. Karl Marx
    c. Konrad Lorenz
    d. Edward O. Wilson

18. In the Marxist view, World War I was
    a. a randomly timed act of warfare.
    b. the product of specific events leading up to it.
    c. a search for new colonies
    d. none of the above

19. An important factor in the effectiveness of antiterrorist policies is
    a. an informed public.
    b. religious tolerance.
    c. visible military presence.
    d. strong leadership.

20. The world's leader in the international sale of weapons is
    a. the United States.
    b. Russia.
    c. Iran.
    d. India.

ESSAY QUESIONS

1. Discuss the theories of Konrad Lorenz and Edward O. Wilson and distinguish between them.

2. Discuss and distinguish the different types of terrorism.

3. Discuss why Lenin thought that the motivation for war would eventually disappear.

4. Discuss the direct and indirect effects of war.

5. Compare and contrast the various theories about war and its origins.

6. Describe how military technology and organization have changed and discuss the impact.

ANSWERS TO MULTIPLE CHOICE QUESTIONS

1.	c	11.	b
2.	c	12.	b
3.	b	13.	d
4.	d	14.	c
5.	c	15.	a
6.	d	16.	b
7.	a	17.	a
8.	d	18.	b
9.	d	19.	b
10.	c	20.	a